SEWING IN A STRAIGHT LINE

SEWING IN A STRAIGHT LINE

quick & crafty **projects** *you can make* **by** simply *sewing straight*

LINE

BRETT BARA

POTTER
CRAFT

NEW YORK

Dedication

for my *mom*.

She taught me to sew, shared with me a love of all things handmade, and even helped me stitch many of the projects for this book. I could never ask for a more wonderful mother.

Copyright © 2011 by Brett Bara

Published in 2011 by Potter Craft,
an imprint of the Crown Publishing Group,
a division of Random House, Inc., New York
www.crownpublishing.com
www.pottercraft.com

POTTER CRAFT and colophon is a
registered trademark of Random House, Inc.

Library of Congress Cataloging-in-Publication Data

Bara, Brett.
Sewing in a straight line : quick and crafty projects
you can make by simply sewing straight / Brett Bara.
    p. cm.
ISBN-13: 978-0-307-58665-0 (pbk.)
ISBN-10: 0-307-58665-0 (pbk.)
tt1. Sewing. 2. Handicraft. I. Title.
 TT705.B225 2011
 646.4--dc22

This book contains general instructions and techniques on sewing clothing, home decor, and craft designs. When working with the tools and supplies presented in this book, readers are strongly cautioned to use proper care and judgment, to follow the applicable manufacturer's directions, and to seek prompt medical attention in case of an injury. In addition, readers are advised to keep all potentially harmful materials away from children. The author and the publisher expressly disclaim any liability, loss, or risk, personal or otherwise, which is incurred as a consequence, directly or indirectly, of the use and application of any of the contents of this book.

Cover and interior design by La Tricia Watford
Cover and interior photography by Alexandra Grablewski
Illustrations by Jane Fay

Printed in China

First printing, 2011

1 2 3 4 5 6 7 8 9 / 19 18 17 16 15 14 13 12 11

Acknowledgments

Writing a book has been a goal of mine for a very long time, and I'm so proud and happy that this dream is finally a reality. I'm beyond thankful to the many people who helped this book come together.

First, I must thank the wonderful crew at Potter Craft who made this vision come to life—*Betty Wong* for supporting me and helping shape my ideas, *Erica Smith* for making the introductions, *Chi Ling Moy* for lending her top-notch aesthetics to the photography, *Martha Moran* for her patient and thoughtful editing, and *La Tricia Watford* for her charming design.

Big thanks to *Alexandra Grablewski* for her gorgeous photographs and *Kristen Petliski* for her excellent styling (as always). Another big thanks goes to *Jordan Provost* and *Jenna Park* (and their families) for welcoming our photo crew into their beautiful homes, and to *Grace Bonney* for introducing us.

It took a team of people to produce this book's projects and whip their patterns into shape. I'm super grateful to *Nikki Smith* for her awesome garment sewing skills and expert advice, *Carol Selepek* for her quilting, and my mom *Arlene Bara* for never complaining that I gave her all the boring parts to sew (who else could bind a quilt in the middle of the night with a smile on her face?). I also want to thank *Don Bara* (or *Dad*, as I like to call him) for his measuring, packing, shipping, and encouraging. I'm very thankful for *Kevin Kosbab's* careful technical editing, and *Jane Fay's* commitment to excellence with her illustrations.

Writing this book has truly made me appreciate all the wonderful people in my life. There aren't enough French dinners in the world to thank *Darren Fried* for being an amazing friend (and also a rock star lawyer). I so appreciate *Erin Slonaker* for sharing her experience listening to me vent, and holding down the crochet fort while I hunkered down and sewed. I'm grateful to *Lanie Kagan* for her kindness and encouragement. And I tip my hat to *Marty*, *Jodie*, *Dan*, *Sara*, *Candi*, and *Lisa* for their friendship and support along the way.

Finally I'd like to thank *my family* and especially *my parents* for all the crafty love while I was working on this book, and always.

contents

straight-up chic fashion 26

cozy, crafty home 76

quick, cute gifts 118

straight to the *point:*

Why Sewing Isn't As Hard As You Think

As a crafty lady living in New York City, I find sewing opportunities everywhere. Just about every time I walk into a trendy boutique, I see something chic and pricey and think, *that's gorgeous—and I could totally make that myself.* Inspiration for cute and stylish creations to sew is all around— and believe it or not, much of it can be made with the most basic skills. If you think sewing your own clothes, home decor, and gifts is too hard, I've got news for you! It's not, and this book will show you why.

The exploding popularity of DIY culture and shows like *Project Runway* have piqued the public's interest in crafting, especially in sewing. I meet so many people who tell me they would love to be able to sew. When writing this book, I frequently heard the same comment: *"I'm dying to learn to sew, but I have no idea where to begin."* I always feel a little sad when I hear this—while it's great that folks out there want to learn, it's a shame they don't realize how easy it is to get started.

I know I'm lucky that I grew up in a crafty house, with a mother who could sew anything and a dad who could build anything. "Making it ourselves" was second nature to our family, so it never occurred to me to be intimidated by sewing machines, fabric, scissors, and patterns. I learned from an early age that sewing isn't difficult at all.

For me, custom home decor, fabulous fashion accessories, funky quilts, and personalized gifts have always been as close as my fabric stash and my sewing machine. And though I've been stitching up challenging constructions for years, the vast majority of what I sew actually uses only the most basic skills. Why? Because many projects simply don't require anything more. In fact, the inspiration for this book was the realization that most of what I sew is made with nothing but *simple straight seams.*

And *anybody* can sew a straight seam—I promise you that.

That's why I want everyone out there to know how simple sewing can be. Sure, you can get all complicated with haute couture gowns or tailor-made suits, but that's not all sewing is. You really don't need fancy techniques to stitch awesome things. If you can sew a straight seam, you can make a world of projects, and this book will take you step-by-step through everything you'll need to know to get the job done. From the basics of sewing (by hand or by machine) to all the helpful tips and tricks you'll need to make everything from curtains, pillows, and quilts to clothes, bags, and toys—it's all just a few easy stitches away!

So grab your needle, break out your scissors, fire up your sewing machine, and don't be afraid—remember, it's only fabric and thread, and the worst that will happen is that you'll tear out your stitches and sew another seam.

With some snazzy textiles, a spare afternoon, a tad of creativity, and this book, you'll soon be jazzing up your life with seriously cute creations. Before long, you'll be seeing inspiration everywhere and thinking, *I can totally make that myself.*

Brett Bara

You really don't need fancy *techniques* to stitch awesome things. If you can sew a *straight* seam, you can make a world of *projects*, and this book will take you step-by-step through everything you'll need to know to *get the job done.*

getting started

HOW TO SEW A STRAIGHT LINE

When you think of it that way—sewing a straight line—it seems so simple, right? Well, it really is that easy! Once you understand the basics of sewing a straight seam, the stitching world is your oyster. It doesn't take long to learn, so let's go over a few basics and then you'll be ready to tackle the projects in this book.

We'll begin with putting together the tools and supplies you'll need and setting up a sewing space. (It doesn't take much, I promise!) I'll then take you step-by-step through the basics of sewing a straight line, by hand and machine, and describe a few essential techniques you'll need for the designs in this book.

If you're a beginning sewer, I suggest you read through this chapter before starting on the projects. Once you start sewing, you may find yourself flipping back to these pages for a reminder or refresher as you work.

SO WHAT ARE WE WAITING FOR? *let's get started!*

basic sewing tools and supplies

Over the years, I've found that one of the most important things I can do to improve my sewing productivity and quality is to have the right tools, and to keep them organized and handy so they'll be ready to go whenever the sewing muse strikes.

You don't need a lot of tools to sew—since I live in New York City, where space is at a minimum, I say no to most gadgets and try to stick to the basics. Here's my minimalist's list of the supplies you'll need to make the projects in this book.

ALL-PURPOSE THREAD: You'll need thread labeled all-purpose, which comes in cotton, polyester, or a blend of both. Choose a color that matches your fabric. (It doesn't need to be an exact match, just close.) When in doubt, choose a shade darker, rather than lighter, than the fabric.

STRAIGHT PINS: Keep a stash of straight pins handy to pin fabrics in place before sewing seams.

HAND-SEWING NEEDLES: Even if you do all of your sewing on the machine, a little hand-sewing is necessary now and then for finishing or detail work. Look for needles called sharps; they come in various sizes for different fabric weights. Stock your sewing kit with a variety pack so you'll be ready for any occasion.

All-purpose thread

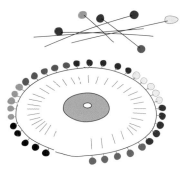

Straight pins

Hand-sewing needles

 *PENNY WISE*

Assembling basic sewing tools doesn't have to break the bank. Ask relatives and friends for loaners to get you started, and check thrift stores and flea markets for affordable supplies.

Remember that many craft-store chains frequently offer fifty-percent-off coupons. Sign up for their mailing lists to receive the coupons regularly, and larger purchases will be more manageable!

SAFETY PINS: Safety pins in a variety of sizes come in handy for tasks such as threading elastic through a waistband casing or holding quilt layers together.

FABRIC-MARKING TOOLS: Sometimes you need to mark your fabric to know where to sew it later. Mark with a nonpermanent tool, such as fabric-marking pencils, disappearing ink pens, water-soluble pens, or tailor's chalk. In a pinch you can use a regular pencil, just be careful to mark inside a seam allowance or other spot where it won't show.

Safety pins

Tailor's chalk

Disappearing ink pen

Fabric-marking pencil

MEASURING TAPES: I keep two types on hand. One is the traditional tailor's tape (also known as a measuring tape), which is flexible cloth or plastic, perfect for measuring around the body; I use it for almost all my sewing needs. The other is a carpenter's retractable metal tape (aka tape measure); it comes in handy for measuring something particularly long and flat, such as curtains or a quilt. (To protect your fabric from stains and dirt, don't use the same metal tape for sewing and home repairs.)

Measuring tape (tailor's tape)

Metal tape measure

SCISSORS: Good, sharp scissors are indispensable. Purchase a decent pair, and reserve them only for fabric—never use them to cut paper or anything else, which will dull the blades.

Sewing scissors

ROTARY CUTTER, CUTTING MAT, AND QUILTER'S RULER: These items are optional, but very useful. I prefer to do most of my cutting with a rotary cutter; it's quicker and more precise than scissors, especially when cutting straight lines.

SEAM RIPPER: Mistakes happen, and when they do, a seam ripper will help remove unwanted stitches easily and without damaging your fabric. This inexpensive tool is also useful for removing basting stitches or opening buttonholes. Like any blade, a seam ripper can get dull, so replace yours often.

POINTER AND CREASER TOOL: Keep a pointy object in your sewing kit for poking out corners after turning them right side out. A knitting needle or chopstick will work, but I prefer using this tool. Its point is small enough to get into little corners but is slightly blunted so you won't risk poking through the fabric.

SEWING MACHINE: You'll only need the most basic of machines to make the projects in this book, but sewing machines are available in a huge array of high- and low-tech choices. Try out various machines in stores to see what you like. Be sure to read your machine's manual to learn how to properly maintain it; if you keep it cleaned and oiled, even a basic machine should last for years. For more information, see page 16.

MACHINE NEEDLES: I'm embarrassed to admit that for many years I didn't appreciate the importance of changing my sewing machine needles. Now I'm enlightened, and I change needles frequently to match the weight of the fabric I'm sewing. (Get yourself an assortment of sizes; the package will tell you which needles work best with which fabrics.) Replace old needles with sharp new ones often.

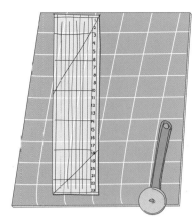

Rotary cutter

Cutting mat and quilter's ruler

Seam ripper

Pointer and creaser tool

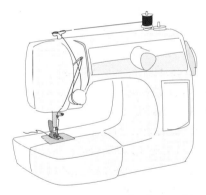

Sewing machine

Machine needles

Iron

Spray bottle

Press cloth

Clapper

Heavy hardcover book

IRON: Believe it or not, an iron is one of the most important tools in sewing. In fact, it might be *the* most important tool. It doesn't matter how nicely you measure, cut, or sew your seams—if they're not pressed flat, they'll look shoddy. Get a good iron and press every seam thoroughly, using steam. (I even recommend ironing topstitching, as it helps to relax the thread and fabric for a more finished look.)

SPRAY BOTTLE AND PRESS CLOTH: I keep a spray bottle of water at my ironing station along with a press cloth, which is just a scrap of muslin fabric. Spritzing fabric before pressing helps achieve smoother results, especially for fabrics that don't want to obey the iron. Placing a press cloth over the fabric you're ironing helps to protect it from scorching or taking on sheen from the iron.

CLAPPER: A clapper is a block of hardwood used to flatten fabric when pressing, especially fabrics that easily burn or melt. Press the fabric with an iron for a few seconds, remove the iron and firmly press the clapper on the same spot. I don't actually own a clapper, but I needed one for the Heavy Metal Bag (page 56), since the vinyl would have melted under normal pressing. I improvised with a hardcover book and it worked just as well!

SEWING SPACE: Sewing requires a place to spread out and work. If you're lucky enough to have a space you can set up as a dedicated sewing area, you're in business. Furnish it with a large, sturdy, stable surface (such as a desk or an old dining table) for cutting fabrics and setting up your machine, as well as some drawers and shelves for supplies.

If you don't have a dedicated space, don't despair! (After all, I don't have one, and I wrote a whole sewing book!) All you need is a good table that you can take over once in a while, and a little bit of organization. Keep your tools and supplies neatly arranged in a plastic bin, which you can easily move from room to room. Store your tools and sewing machine in an accessible spot.

sewing a straight line: by hand

If you're itching to dive into the wonderful world of fabric, creativity, and DIY flair, you don't need a sewing machine to get started. Sew by hand! It may be slow going, but hand-sewing can be wonderfully meditative and relaxing. Nearly every project in this book can be made by hand, and all you need is a hand-sewing needle, all-purpose thread, and sharp scissors. Here's the low-down on the basics you'll need to know.

THREADING THE NEEDLE: Cut a thread length about 40" (100cm) long and thread one end through the eye of the needle. To sew with a single thread, knot one end. To sew with two strands, knot both ends together. FIGURE 1)

basic hand stitches

Most seams are sewn with fabric placed right sides together and raw edges aligned. Pin before sewing so the fabric doesn't shift. To begin a stitch, insert the needle from the back of the fabric up to the front.

THE BACKSTITCH creates a strong seam which is the best choice for basic hand sewing. To make each stitch, insert the needle into the preceding stitch, then bring the needle up where the next stitch will be placed.

THE RUNNING STITCH (straight stitch) is a basic stitch which is less stable than the back stitch. Simply weave the needle in and out through both layers of fabric for the length of the seam.

THE HAND-BASTING STITCH is a long (approximately ½" [13mm]) running stitch, used to secure fabric layers before sewing the permanent seam.

THE WHIPSTITCH is a loop-shaped stitch that can be used to join two fabric edges together or to sew a hem. Insert the needle from the back to the front about ¼" (6mm) from the fabric edges, then insert the needle from front to back so the thread wraps around the edges.

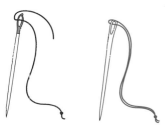

tip

Trouble threading the needle? Simply snip the thread with sharp scissors, moisten it with wet fingers, and thread it through the eye of the needle. If that doesn't work, moisten (okay, *lick*!) the eye of the needle itself. It sounds crazy, but a wet needle eye helps wick the thread through.

FIGURE 1

Backstitch

Running stitch

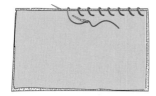

Whipstitch on an edge

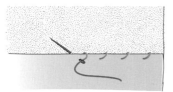

Whipstitch a hem

sewing a straight line: by machine

Here comes the million-dollar question: What kind of sewing machine do you need? Well, I'm a big fan of nonfancy models. These days sewing machines can be really complicated, but I highly recommend that beginners start with inexpensive or mid-range machines.

Before you buy, consider borrowing. There are sewing machines lying neglected in closets everywhere—ask around and you may find a loaner you can enjoy until you're ready to buy. If in doubt about a borrowed machine, take it to a sewing machine repair shop for a tune-up or assessment.

If borrowing isn't an option, check your local listings for sewing machine shops that rent models. In some cities there are businesses that allow you to rent a sewing station or even cutting space by the hour—these can be really fun spots for meeting fellow sewers, learning new skills, and getting tons of inspiration.

Finally, if you do buy, know that sewing machine dealers are set up to let you experiment with machines before purchasing. Don't be shy about testing out the various models until you find just the right one for you.

getting started on a machine

Sewing a straight line is without doubt the easiest thing you can do with your sewing machine. Because all models are different, you will have to get to know your own machine to understand how to operate it. It's critical to read the manual; it will really help you to understand your machine's functions and get the most out of it.

If you don't know your way around a sewing machine, I encourage you to take a class at a local sewing shop, or ask a friend or relative for lessons. It really only takes a few hours to learn the basics, and then you'll be on your way!

basic machine stitches

Here are the basic straight sewing stitches. Practice these stitches with various stitch lengths on scrap fabrics to get the hang of each one.

THE STRAIGHT STITCH, a line of straight stitches, is the most basic machine stitch—the one you will use whenever a pattern simply tells you to sew. Check your machine's manual for the stitch-length setting you should use for general sewing.

BACKSTITCH at the beginning and end of the seam to prevent it from unraveling. Sew a couple stitches forward then press the backstitch button (or lever) to make the machine to go in reverse. Sew a couple stitches in reverse, release the button, and continue sewing normally. This is the machine equivalent of tying a knot.

TOPSTITCH is just a fancy name for a basic straight stitch that is visible on the right side of your work, usually a decorative element near a finished edge.

A BASTING STITCH temporarily holds fabric together at the seam line until the permanent seam is sewn. Use your longest machine stitch length. Do not backstitch at the beginning or end so you can easily remove the basting stitches.

A ZIGZAG STITCH is just what it sounds like, a z-shaped stitch that zigs and zags. Most sewing machines have a zigzag setting, and you can usually adjust the width and length of the stitches. Zigzags are most frequently used to finish a raw edge or as a decorative stitch.

Straight stitch

Backstitch

Topstitch

Basting stitch

Zigzag stitch

basic sewing techniques

Learn these basic sewing techniques and you'll be able to make every project in this book. If something is new to you, practice first on scrap fabric and don't get frustrated if you don't get it right the first time. That's why seam rippers were invented.

french seam

A French seam is a two-step seam that is fully finished on both the inside and the outside of your work, so no raw edges are visible. It may sound intimidating, but it's really no more difficult than a regular seam, and you'll love the professional-looking results. Note that a ¼" (6mm) French seam refers to the width of the *finished* seam; the actual seam allowance is ½" (13mm). To sew a ¼" (6mm) French seam:

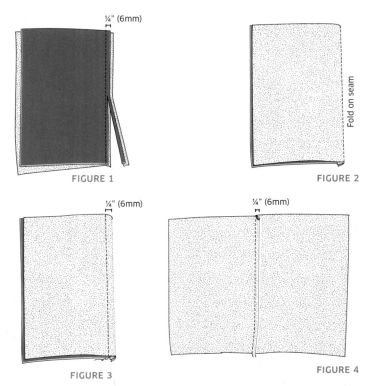

¼" (6mm)

FIGURE 1

Fold on seam

FIGURE 2

¼" (6mm)

FIGURE 3

¼" (6mm)

FIGURE 4

1. Pin 2 pieces of fabric with their *wrong* sides together and raw edges aligned. (This will feel wrong, since normally seams are sewn with right sides together, but trust me!) Stitch the seam with a ¼" (6mm) seam allowance. Trim seam allowance to ¹/₈" (3mm). (FIGURE 1)

2. Press the seam allowance to one side, then fold the fabric along the seam line so the *right* sides of the fabric are together. Press the seam on the fold; pin. (FIGURE 2)

3. Sew another seam with a ¼" (6mm) seam allowance, enclosing the raw edge of the first seam (Step 2) inside this new seam, leaving a finished, encased seam on the wrong side. (FIGURE 3)

4. Press the seam allowance to one side, and your beautiful French seam is done! (FIGURE 4)

trimming corners

When you sew something that has a corner (which will then be turned right side out), you will be instructed to trim the seam allowance from the corner. To do this, simply cut off the corner seam allowance at a 45-degree angle, being careful not to cut too close to the stitching. In very tight situations or when using heavy fabric, you can also trim some of the seam allowance beyond the corner. By removing the bulk of the excess fabric, you will get a sharper turned-out corner.

Trimmed corner

stitch in the ditch

At times, patterns will instruct you to "stitch in the ditch". This means you'll sew directly over an existing seam to anchor something beneath the seam, such as the elastic in a waistband. Simply lower your sewing machine needle into the existing seam, and sew along in the "ditch" over the previous stitching.

Stitch in the ditch

fusing interfacing

To give a fabric more body and strength in places where it's needed (such as straps and buttonholes), you can add fusible interfacing to the wrong side of the fabric.

Cut the interfacing to the dimensions specified in the pattern. Place the fabric wrong side up on your ironing board and place the interfacing adhesive side down on the fabric. With your iron set to high, press the interfacing one spot at a time, holding the iron in place for 5–10 seconds before moving to the next area. Check to see if the adhesive has bonded; if it hasn't, press each section again using a damp press cloth.

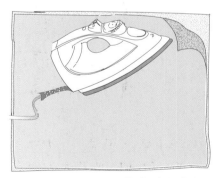

Fusing interfacing

making a strap

This type of strap is used in several projects in this book. Here's how to make it.

FIGURE 1

FIGURE 2

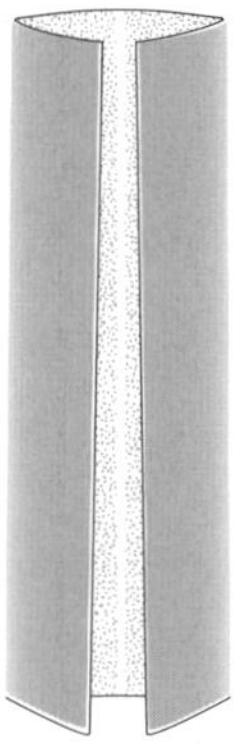

FIGURE 3 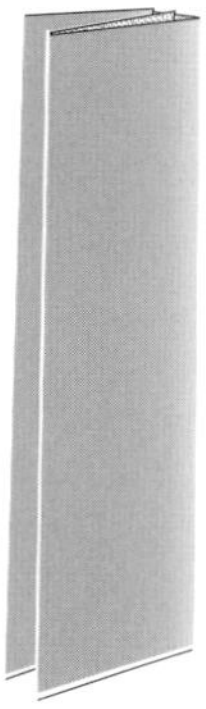   FIGURE 4 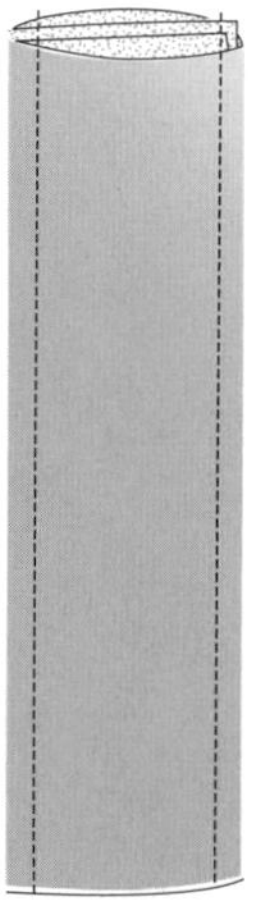   FIGURE 5

getting started

1. Cut a strip of fabric (on the lengthwise grain) that is 4 times wider than you want your strap to be. (FIGURE 1)

2. Fold the strip in half lengthwise (wrong sides together) and press it. (FIGURE 2)

3. Open the strip with the wrong side facing up, and fold the 2 long edges in to meet at the center (folded) line. (FIGURE 3) Press in place.

4. Fold the entire strip in half on the original fold line so the raw edges are inside, and press again. (FIGURE 4)

5. Topstitch along both long edges of the strap, stitching close to the folds. (FIGURE 5)

basting a quilt

To prepare for quilting, you'll assemble all the layers of a quilt (top, batting, and back) and secure them together so they don't shift during the quilting process. Some quilters use safety pins, but I find it works best to hand-baste the layers together with needle and thread—don't worry, it doesn't take as long as you think.

Thread a hand-sewing needle and make very long stitches (approximately 2" [5cm]) across the quilt. Place the next line of stitches about 6" (15cm) from the first, and continue sewing lines of stitches in a grid pattern until the entire quilt is basted.

quilting a quilt

Once you've basted your quilt, you will quilt the layers together to firmly secure them for durability while giving your piece the distinctive look that makes a quilt, well, quilty. To quilt by hand, simply sew basic running stitches (page 15) across the entire quilt, spacing the lines of quilting no more than 6" (15cm) apart. You can also quilt on your sewing machine, which is my preferred method. Check your sewing machine manual for instructions on how to adjust your machine for quilting or sewing thick fabrics, and practice a few lines of quilting on a small swatch of your fabrics and batting layered together, adjusting the stitch length to be sure you are happy with the result. If you have a very large piece to quilt, consider using a quilting service to do the job (your fabric store can probably suggest a local service).

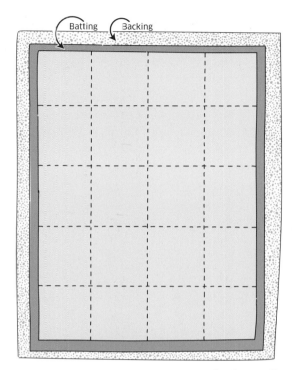

Batting   Backing

Basting a quilt

21

binding a quilt

All that's left to do after a quilt has been quilted is to finish the raw edges around the perimeter. To do this, a special strip of folded fabric, called quilt binding, is stitched to the edges. Here's how to make and attach ½" (13mm) quilt binding.

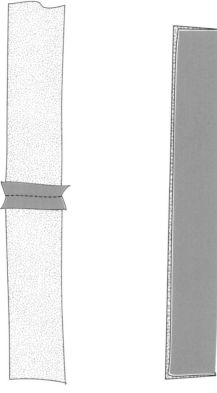

FIGURE 1   FIGURE 2

making quilt binding

1. Cut 3"- (7.5cm-) wide strips of fabric as long as the perimeter of your quilt, plus about 12" (30.5cm) extra for seam allowances. You will likely have to cut several strips to achieve the necessary length. Many sources call for these strips to be cut on the bias, but for binding straight-sided items like quilts, I find that strips cut with the grain work just fine.

2. With right sides together, join the strips into one continuous length. Place one strip on top of the other aligning the short edges; pin. Sew them together with a ¼" (6mm) seam allowance and press the seam allowance open. Continue until all strips are joined. (FIGURE 1)

3. Fold the entire strip in half lengthwise (wrong sides together), pressing as you fold. (FIGURE 2)

attaching quilt binding

4. Beginning in the center of one side of the quilt, align both raw edges of the folded binding strip with the raw edges of the quilt; pin. Sew in place with a ½" (13mm) seam allowance. (FIGURE 3)

5. When you reach a corner, here's how to turn it:

   Sew until you are ½" (13mm) from the corner of the quilt. Backstitch (page 17) and cut the thread. (FIGURE 4)

   Fold the binding so it is perpendicular to itself. (FIGURE 5) Holding the folded edge in place, fold the binding again so that the raw edges of the folded binding meet the raw edge of the next side of the quilt. (FIGURE 6)

   Lower the machine needle into the binding and quilt layers at the corner and sew along this side of the quilt until you reach the next corner (FIGURE 7), then repeat step 5.

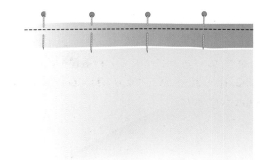

FIGURE 3

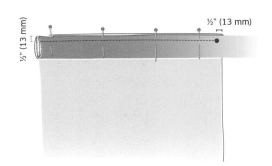

FIGURE 4

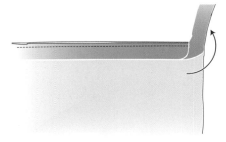

FIGURE 5

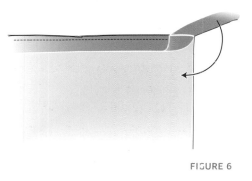

FIGURE 6

FIGURE 7

finishing quilt binding

6. When you've sewn around all 4 corners, stop your seam about 12" (30.5cm) before you reach the point where you began attaching the binding. Remove the quilt from the machine, and trim the binding strip to about 3" (7.5cm) past the point where you began attaching the binding. (FIGURE 8)

7. Fold the end of the binding at a 45-degree angle and press. Return the quilt to the machine and pick up sewing where you left off, stitching all the way to the folded end of the strip. (FIGURE 9)

8. Fold the binding over the raw edge to the *back* side of the quilt. (FIGURE 10) Whipstitch (page 15) the folded edge of the binding to the quilt back (FIGURE 11) and at the join of the binding, making your stitches as small as possible.

12" (30.5cm)

FIGURE 8

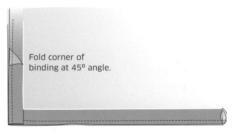

Fold corner of binding at 45° angle.

FIGURE 9

FIGURE 10

FIGURE 11

fabric basics

Before you purchase fabric for your projects, you should understand some fabric properties and terminology.

FABRIC WIDTH: The yardage recommendations in the projects' supplies lists are based on 45"- (115cm-) wide fabric. However, fabric is sometimes sold in other widths. If you purchase a width other than 45" (115cm), take care to double-check the sizes of the fabric pieces you need to cut to make sure you're buying enough.

THE RIGHT SIDE of the fabric is the side that will show on your finished piece. Fabric prints, texture, and surface characteristics (like luster and sheen) are on the right side.

THE WRONG SIDE of the fabric is the side that will be on the inside of your project.

preshrinking

If your fabric is machine washable, I recommend washing and drying it before sewing to preshrink the fibers. If you skip this step, your finished item could bunch at the seams or not fit properly after being washed. If you don't intend to launder an item (for nonwashable items such as The Magic Sewing Kit [page 134], for example) you don't need to worry about preshrinking.

grain

If you look closely at a woven fabric, you'll see it's made up of fine threads woven in a grid pattern, with shorter crosswise threads that weave under and over longer lengthwise threads.

THE SELVAGE is the narrow finished border that runs along both long edges of the fabric as it comes off the bolt. This is where the crosswise threads change direction during the weaving process.

LENGTHWISE GRAIN refers to the threads that run parallel to the selvage edges and have little stretch or give, which is why most fabrics are cut on the lengthwise grain. Cut all length measurements on the lengthwise grain.

CROSSWISE GRAIN refers to the shorter threads that run perpendicular to the selvage edges; these threads have more stretch and give than lengthwise threads. Cut all width measurements on the crosswise grain.

BIAS GRAIN is the diagonal intersection of the lengthwise and crosswise threads and has a lot of stretch.

 CUTTING LARGE FABRIC PIECES

It can be tricky to cut large pieces of fabric evenly. Here are some tips that might help when you are cutting large items such as curtain and quilt pieces.

* Use the selvage edge of the fabric as a guide, and make the first cut parallel to this edge. Base subsequent cuts on this first one to keep the cutting lines straight.
* When working with very large pieces, fold the fabric, aligning the selvage edge with itself, and cut through several layers at once.
* Use a large cutting mat and rotary cutter; the lines on these tools really help to keep the fabric straight.
* When working with very large pieces, I use a carpenter's laser T-square to mark straight lines on my fabric and make perfect corners on my quilts.

straight-up chic fashion

Think you need fancy skills to **sew stylish clothes**? I'm here to tell you that that's simply not true! You can sew a wide array of basic pieces using—you guessed it—**straight lines** only.

The secret is in the fabric you choose. Look for fabrics that drape well (such as knits or sheers), which will give even the simplest garments a *flattering shape*. Or choose bold, *eye-catching prints*, which allow the fabric to be the star in an otherwise basic piece.

The *projects* in this chapter are guaranteed to *look great* and *teach* you tons of skills. If you're a beginner, start with the One-Hour Skirt or the Shirred to the Max dress (they're both simple tubes with a little elastic in the right places), or the 60-Second Belt—it's the epitome of instant *DIY gratification*!

Check out the Easy, Breezy Blouse to work with a delicate sheer fabric, or the First Time's a Charm Cardi, a comfy knit garment that's easy even if you've never sewn with knits. *Try your hand* at the City Girl Tote to learn the basics of bag construction, or stitch Quilty Zigs and Zags, a striking quilted belt that's super easy to *personalize*.

For a challenge, don't miss the Origami Dress, a sweet, swingy number that features an intricate pleated trim. Work with a demanding material in the Heavy Metal Bag—a studded, faux-leather purse that *no one* will believe you made yourself. The Sewing School Skirt is a tailoring tutorial that will show you the ins and outs of making a fitted waistband, pleats, and buttonholes.

You can *customize* each of the garments to your own body size for a fit that's sure to flatter. Before you begin, take your body measurements (or better, have a friend take them) and write them down. If you have doubts about any project, sew a muslin sample first to gain a firm *understanding* of the construction process and work out any kinks related to size, fit, and sewing techniques.

Sound like fun? It is! And I promise that sewing your own clothes isn't as tricky as you might think. *Let's get started!*

the one-hour *skirt*

When you see how easy it is to sew your own **quick** and **comfy** skirt you won't ever want to purchase this wardrobe basic off the rack again. With just one yard of fabric and a mere sixty minutes, you can **whip up** a fantastic little number that looks like a million bucks. You can easily adapt this pattern to make a variety of different looks—try a narrower elastic waist, a longer length, or even less gathering to suit your own personal style.

finished dimensions
WIDTH: Sized to fit your body
LENGTH: 18" (45.5cm)

supplies
* Basic sewing supplies (page 11)
* Approximately 1 yard (91cm) medium weight fabric (see Note)
* 1¾"- (4.5cm-) wide elastic (the length of your waist circumference)
* One large safety pin

fabric suggestions
I made this skirt in a cotton-linen blend, which is soft and has great drape. Almost any light or medium weight fabric will work for this project; just keep in mind that the texture of the fabric you choose will determine whether your skirt is flowy or more structured.

note
This garment is sized to fit your measurements so the exact amount of fabric needed will vary. Read the entire pattern and take your body measurements (Step 1) to determine the exact amount you'll need. Buy extra when in doubt.

1. measure + cut

FABRIC: Measure your hip circumference (7"–8" [18cm–20.5cm] below your natural waist, or at your widest point) for measurement **A**. Cut 2 rectangles with a width equal to **A** and a length of 22½" (57cm). **(FIGURE 1)**

ELASTIC: Measure your waist circumference and cut a piece of elastic to that measurement minus 1" (2.5cm).

2. sew the side seams

Pin then sew the 2 front/back pieces together along both 22½" (57cm) edges with ¼" (6mm) French seams (page 18). **(FIGURE 2)**

3. sew the waistband casing

Turn under the top edge ½" (13mm); press. Turn under this folded top edge 2" (5cm); press then pin. Topstitch (page 17) the folded edge in place, leaving a 4" (10cm) opening near one of the side seams. **(FIGURE 3)**

4. sew the hem

Turn under the hem ½" (13mm); press. Turn it under again 1½" (3.8cm); press then pin. Topstitch the hem in place.

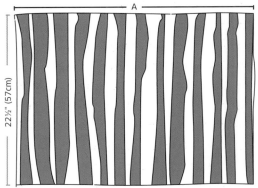

Front/Back (cut 2)

FIGURE 1

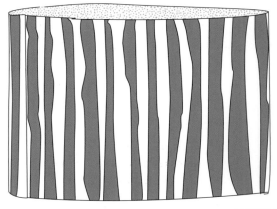

FIGURE 2

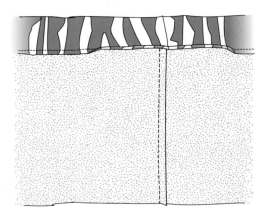

FIGURE 3

5. *finish the waistband*

Attach a safety pin to one end of the elastic and thread that end through the entire waistband casing, being careful not to twist the elastic. When the safety pin gets back to the opening, overlap the 2 raw edges of the elastic ½" (13mm) and sew them together with a straight stitch (page 17), backstitching (page 17) to reinforce at the beginning and end of the seam. Insert the joined elastic ends back into the casing. Topstitch the opening of the casing closed.

Distribute the gathers evenly around the skirt. Once the gathers are arranged, stitch in the ditch (page 19) along each side seam at the waistband to secure the elastic in place.

 GO CUSTOM

You can change this pattern up in lots of ways to make whatever kind of skirt your heart desires. Here are a few options.

* If you prefer the look of a skinny waistband, just use thinner elastic and adjust the waistband casing accordingly. (Make the casing ¼" [6mm] wider than the elastic.)
* This skirt measures 18" (45.5cm) from waist to hem. To make it longer or shorter (if you dare!), just adjust the length of the rectangle you cut in Step 1. (You may need to buy more fabric for a longer skirt.)
* The fabric you choose has a huge impact on the look of this garment. A very light fabric with a lot of drape will give you a flowy skirt; choose something stiff like taffeta for a poufy ball-gown effect.

quilty *zigs and zags*

Add a little crafty flair to your look with this ***graphic belt***.
The layers of free-form quilting are ***easy and fun*** to do, but
if you prefer a different look, you can make this belt with a
patterned fabric and keep the quilting more minimal. I love
that this belt ***makes a big statement***, yet it's made from soft
materials that are comfortable enough to wear all day. even if
you sit at a desk. Anything that's ***cute and comfortable*** is a
winner in my book!

finished dimensions
WIDTH: 2¼" (5.5cm)
LENGTH: Sized to fit your body

supplies
* Basic sewing supplies (page 11)
* ¼ yard (23cm) solid medium-weight cotton
* ¼ yard (23cm) medium-loft cotton quilt batting
* All-purpose thread to match fabric
* All-purpose threads (in 2 colors) to contrast with fabric
* Belt buckle with 2" (5cm) opening and center bar

fabric suggestions
Quilting cottons are perfect for this belt;
almost any medium-weight woven would
work too.

GETTING CLOSURE

Where to find the perfect buckle? I chose this
one from the legendary M&J Trimming in New
York City (mjtrim.com). Try checking your local
trimming shops, but better yet, keep your eyes
peeled at thrift stores and flea markets; you
may find an old belt with a cool buckle that's
worth recycling. Etsy.com has a great selection
of crafty buckles, too.

1. measure + cut
Measure your body at your true waist. Add 10"
(25.5cm) to this number for measurement **A**.

FABRIC: Cut 2 strips of fabric 2¾" (7cm) wide
and as long as **A** (if your fabric isn't long
enough to accommodate **A**, piece 2 strips of
fabric together).

BATTING: Cut one strip of batting the same size
as the fabric. minus 4" (10cm) in length.

2. *sew the layers together*

Layer both pieces of fabric *right sides together*, aligning all raw edges. Place the batting on top of the layered fabric, aligned at one 2¾" (7cm) end. Cut this end (through the batting and both fabric layers) at an angle to form the slanted end of the belt. (Aim for a 45-degree angle, but it doesn't have to be perfect.) Pin all 3 layers together.

Using thread to match your fabric, sew around 3 sides with a ¼" (6mm) seam allowance. Leave the *unslanted* end open. **(FIGURE 1)**

Carefully trim the seam allowance to approximately ⅛" (3mm). Trim the excess fabric and batting from the points of the corners (page 19). Turn the piece right side out so that both pieces of fabric are outside and the batting is inside. Use a pointy tool to gently poke out the corners.

Press the belt thoroughly, using your fingers to spread the seams flat and open as you go.

Turn under the remaining raw edges ¼" (6mm) to the inside. Press. Topstitch (page 17) near the fold to close the end.

straight-up chic fashion

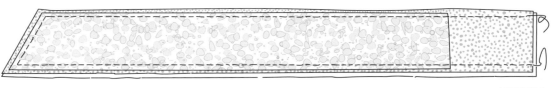

FIGURE 1

FIGURE 2

3. quilt the belt

Adjust your machine's stitch length to a quilting length; I recommend 8 stitches per inch (3mm-long stitches). Using contrasting thread and a straight stitch, and beginning at one end of the belt, simply sew a random zigzagging line all the way to the other end of the belt. Make 4 passes in the first color of thread, alternating between sharp and wide angles. Change to a different color thread and make one more pass. (FIGURE 2)

4. attach the buckle

Wrap the straight end of belt around the center post of the buckle. By hand, whipstitch (page 15) the end to the body of the belt 1" (2.5cm) from the post of the buckle.

 PERFECTLY RANDOM

Sometimes it's tricky to get that perfectly unplanned look in a project. I got my uneven zigzag effect here by layering several free-form passes of quilting stitches. I varied the width of each zig and zag without premeditation, and I also varied the point at which each zig and zag turned. If you look closely you can see that some points reach almost to the edge of the belt, while others don't extend quite so far. That's all there is to it—so let go of all planning and just wing it on this one, for an end result that's all you!

35

quilty zigs and zags

36

straight-up chic fashion

shirred to the max

Would you believe me if I said this maxi dress is a *snap to make*? A super easy technique called shirring creates the fitted bodice, *transforming* a plain rectangle *into a fitted*, flattering *garment*—like magic! Add a bold print, and you've got a major statement dress that you can stitch up in just a couple hours. And if strapless isn't your thing, *no worries*—you can add straps in a snap.

finished dimensions
Sized to fit your body

supplies
* Basic sewing supplies (page 11)
* Approximately 3 yards (2.7m) lightweight cotton fabric (see Note)
* Elastic thread

fabric suggestions
Very light cottons, such as voile, are ideal to achieve a soft, floaty silhouette.

1. ## *measure + cut*
   BUST: Measure your bust circumference and add 1" (2.5cm) for measurement A

   DRESS LENGTH: Measure your desired dress length and add 2" (5cm) for measurement B.

   Cut 2 rectangles that are as wide as A and as long as B. (FIGURE 1)

note

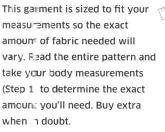

This garment is sized to fit your measurements so the exact amount of fabric needed will vary. Read the entire pattern and take your body measurements (Step 1) to determine the exact amount you'll need. Buy extra when in doubt.

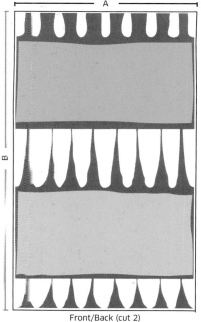

Front/Back (cut 2)

FIGURE 1

2. sew the front and back

Pin then sew the front and back pieces together along one of the long sides with a ¼" (6mm) French seam (page 18) to form one large rectangle. **(FIGURE 2)**

3. hem and mark the top

Turn under the top edge ½" (13mm); press. Turn the folded edge under ½" (13mm) again; press. Topstitch (page 17) the hem in place.

Lay the dress so the right side is facing up. Beginning ¾" (2cm) from the top edge, use chalk or a disappearing ink pen to draw lines parallel to the top edge spaced ¾" (2cm) apart. Draw as many lines as you would like rows of gathering; more lines will create a more fitted bodice. For the dress shown here, 8 rows were drawn. **(FIGURE 2)**

4. shirr the bodice

Hand-wind the elastic thread onto an empty bobbin. Add a *little bit* of tension as you wind. Don't worry too much about getting it perfect; just make sure there are no knots and the thread is somewhat evenly wound on the bobbin. Load the bobbin into your machine as you normally would. Use all-purpose thread in the needle. With the fabric right side up, sew along the marked lines on your dress, starting with the line nearest the top edge. Backstitch (page 17) at the beginning and end of each shirred row. The elastic thread will automatically create the gathers as you sew; at first the fabric may not gather very much, but as you sew more rows the gathering will increase. Stretch out the fabric as you work to keep it flat as you stitch each line. After sewing the lines of shirring, steam the

tip

If strapless isn't your style, add straps by stitching ribbon to the inside top edge, or make narrow straps (page 20) from your fabric.

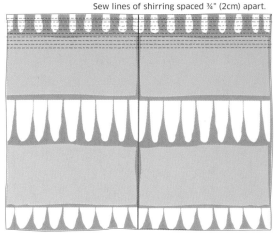

Sew lines of shirring spaced ¾" (2cm) apart.

FIGURE 2

fabric by holding a steam iron just above the shirring, which will cause the shirring to bunch up. Do not press the iron on the shirring, or you will flatten it.

5. *sew the remaining side seam*

Pin then sew the dress's remaining long edges together with a ¼" (6mm) French seam. Make sure the top and bottom edges and shirred rows are all aligned. **(FIGURE 3)**

6. *hem the skirt*

Turn under the hem ½" (13mm) and press. Turn it under again 1" (2.5cm) and press. Topstitch the hem in place close. **(FIGURE 3)**

 SHIRR GENIUS

Simply by replacing your normal bobbin thread with elastic thread, you can create a gathered effect that is comfy and flattering to boot.

On this dress, you can work the shirring to just below the bustline, extend it a little lower to flatter the midriff, or work it all the way to the waistline.

Practice on some scrap fabric just to get the hang of it. Here are some pointers to get you started.

* Hand wind the elastic thread around your bobbin; it won't work on the machine. Wind with a little tension, but not too much.
* Mark the shirr lines before sewing, or use your presser foot to space them.
* Backstitch securely at the beginning and end of each line.
* You won't see much gathering at first but don't fret. The more lines you sew, the more your fabric will pucker.
* After shirring, blast your fabric with a steam iron (held 1 inch [2.5cm] above the shirring) to see it pucker up even more.
* Try this technique on sleeve cuffs and necklines.

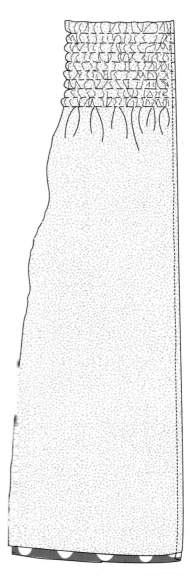

FIGURE 3

easy, breezy *blouse*

When *designing* this top, I wanted to show that even the most basic garment could look *sophisticated* if stitched in the right fabric. I used a high-end silk chiffon to transform a simple boxy shape into a dreamy, *fluid silhouette* that's light as air—and the end result is truly greater than the sum of its parts. Sewing chiffon can be a challenge, so this basic top is the perfect starting project if you're new to sheer materials.

finished dimensions

WIDTH: Sized to fit your body
LENGTH: 25" (63.5cm)

supplies

* Basic sewing supplies (page 11)
* Approximately 1½ yards (1.4m) silk or polyester chiffon (see Note on page 42)

1. *measure + cut*

FRONT AND BACK: Measure the width of your body from shoulder to shoulder and add 6" (15cm) for measurement **A**. Cut 2 rectangles with the width of **A** and 26" (66cm) long. (If you prefer a different length than the one shown here, measure from your shoulder to the length you want and add 1" [2.5cm] for seam allowances, and cut your rectangle to this length.) (FIGURE 1)

WORKING WITH CHIFFON

If this is your first time working with chiffon, I suggest buying a little more fabric than you need. Use the extra to practice cutting, sewing seams, and hemming—you'll be a pro in no time!

Sheer fabrics like chiffon can be difficult to cut straight, but they often tear easily in a straight line. Test on your fabric first to make sure you get the results you want, and then cut out your rectangles by snipping the fabric and gently pulling the fabric at the snip to tear it. Don't worry, it's not as scary as it sounds.

Front/Back (cut 2)

FIGURE 1

note

This garment is sized to fit your measurements so the exact amount of fabric needed will vary. Read the entire pattern and take your body measurements (Step 1) to determine the exact amount you'll need. Buy extra when in doubt.

SLEEVES: Cut 2 rectangles 26" (66cm) long and 24" (61cm) wide for the sleeves. (This creates a very wide sleeve; if you prefer, you can customize the sleeve to a different width. Loop a tape measure loosely around your upper arm to determine the width you prefer, and cut to this measurement plus 1" [2.5cm] for seam allowances.) **(FIGURE 2)**

24" (61cm)

26" (66cm)

Sleeve (cut 2)

FIGURE 2

2. *sew shoulder seams*

With wrong sides together, pin the front to the back with the top raw edges aligned. Sew the shoulder seams with a ¼" (6mm) French seam (page 18). Start stitching at each side edge and continue for 5" (12.5cm), leaving the center of the top edge open for the neck. Press the seam allowances to the back. **(FIGURE 3)**

5" (12.5cm)   5" (12.5cm)

FIGURE 3

3. attach the sleeves

Lay the joined front/back piece wrong side up on a flat surface. With wrong sides together, pin one sleeve to the front/back, centering a 24" (61cm) edge over the shoulder seam, aligning raw edges (FIGURE 4). Sew the sleeve to the top with a ¼" (6mm) French seam. Press the seam allowance toward the sleeve. Repeat for the remaining sleeve.

4. sew side seams

Fold the top at the shoulder seams, wrong sides together, aligning the underarm and side edges. Sew from the bottom up the side seams and along the arms with ¼" (6mm) French seams. (FIGURE 5)

5 hem the neck, sleeves, and bottom edge

To create a narrow hem on sheer fabric, work as follows: First topstitch ¼" (6mm) from the fabric's raw edge, then turn under the hem along the stitching and press (FIGURE 6).

Stitch again about ⅛" (3mm) from the fold, stitching through both layers. Carefully trim the hem allowance as close to the second stitching line as you can. (FIGURE 7)

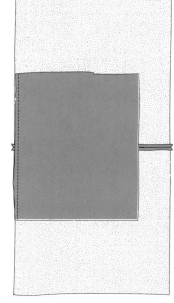

FIGURE 4

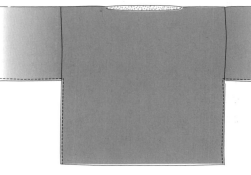

FIGURE 5

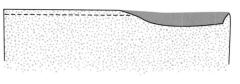

FIGURE 6

FIGURE 7

Turn up the hem once more along the second stitching line and press. Topstitch close to the upper folded edge (a scant ⅛" [3mm] from the outer edge) and press. (FIGURE 8)

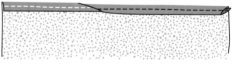

FIGURE 8

Using ½" (13mm) hem allowances and the method described above, make a narrow hem along the neckline and the bottom edge. Try on the top and mark how long you want the sleeves. Make sure they are equal. If necessary, trim each sleeve ½" (13mm) below your marked length and make a narrow hem around each sleeve opening.

city girl *tote*

city girl *tote*

Here in **New York**, tote bags are an essential for city ladies. I never leave my apartment without one, and every day my **bag** is stuffed with everything from my lunch, makeup, and a change of shoes to a **craft project**, a water bottle, and who knows what else. Whew—I get tired just thinking about everything we carry around, but an adorable bag makes it much more bearable. If you're a basic dresser, there's no better way to add some *pizzazz* to your look than with a cute tote. If you **love** fabric, totes are the perfect use for snazzy textiles.

finished dimensions
WIDTH: 19" (48.5cm)
HEIGHT (excluding strap): 15" (38cm)

supplies
* Basic sewing supplies (page 11)
* 1 yard (91cm) heavyweight fabric (for exterior)
* 1 yard (91cm) medium-heavy fabric (for lining and straps)
* 1 yard (91cm) heavyweight fusible interfacing
* 5 yards (4.6m) ½"- (13mm-) wide metallic trim
* All-purpose thread to match your fabrics
* All-purpose thread to contrast with your fabrics

fabric suggestions
Heavy fabrics such as canvas or cotton duck will make a nice, sturdy tote. I suggest a medium-heavy fabric for the lining, such as cotton twill.

1. **measure + cut**

BODY EXTERIOR AND INTERFACING: Cut one 32" x 20" (81cm x 51cm) rectangle from the exterior fabric. Find the center point of each long edge, and cut a centered 3" x 5" (7.5cm x 12.5cm) rectangle from each side. Cut one piece the same size and shape from the interfacing. **(FIGURE 1)**

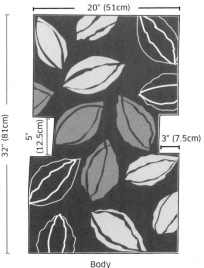

Body
Exterior Fabric (cut 1)
Interfacing (cut 1)

FIGURE 1

LINING: Cut one 26" x 20" (66cm x 51cm) rectangle from the lining fabric. Find the center point of the long edge and cut a 3" x 5" (7.5cm x 12.5cm) rectangle from each side, just as you did for the exterior.

FACING: Cut two 4" x 20" (10cm x 51cm) pieces from the exterior fabric and 2 from the interfacing.

STRAPS: Cut two 6" x 30" (15 cm x 76cm) pieces from the lining fabric and 2 from the interfacing. (FIGURE 2)

2. *attach interfacing*

Using a steam iron, fuse the interfacing pieces (page 19) to the wrong sides of the corresponding exterior and facing pieces.

3. *sew the tote exterior*

Fold the tote exterior in half with right sides together and short edges aligned; pin. Sew side seams with a ½" (13mm) seam allowance. (FIGURE 3) Press the seam allowances open. Fold the corners flat, centering the side seams; pin. Stitch closed with a ½" (13mm) seam allowance. (FIGURE 3 INSET) Trim the corners (page 19), turn the tote right side out, and use a pointy tool to carefully poke out the corners. Press the seams.

4. *sew the facing and lining*

With right sides together and aligning all edges, pin then sew a facing piece to each short edge of the lining with a ½" (13mm) seam allowance. Press the seam allowance toward the facing.

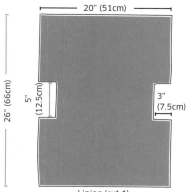

20" (51cm)

26" (66cm)

5" (12.5cm)

3" (7.5cm)

Lining (cut 1)

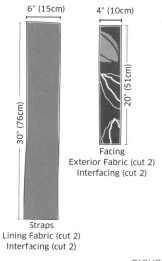

6" (15cm)

4" (10cm)

30" (76cm)

20" (51cm)

Facing
Exterior Fabric (cut 2)
Interfacing (cut 2)

Straps
Lining Fabric (cut 2)
Interfacing (cut 2)

FIGURE 2

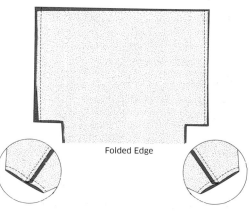

Folded Edge

FIGURE 3

Fold the entire piece in half with right sides together and the raw edges of the facing aligned; pin. Sew the side seams with a ½" (13mm) seam allowance, leaving a 6" (15cm) opening in the *center* of one side seam. (FIGURE 4) Sew the corners closed; trim, turn, and press them as you did for the exterior in Step 3.

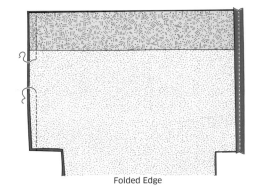

Folded Edge

FIGURE 4

5. *attach the lining to the bag*

With the lining inside out, the tote exterior right side out, and with *right sides together*, place the tote exterior inside the lining, aligning the side seams and top raw edges; pin. Sew the exterior and facing together at the top raw edges with a ½" (13mm) seam allowance. Turn right side out, carefully turning the tote through the opening in the side seam of the lining.

Extend the lining above the bag and press the seam allowance toward the facing. Turn the lining inside the bag and press the folded top edge where the facing meets the exterior. Topstitch (page 17) the upper edge of the tote, sewing close to the edge.

Whipstitch (page 15) the opening in the lining closed.

6. *make straps*

Using the strap pieces cut in Step 1, make 2 straps following the directions on page 20.

Cut four 30" (76cm) lengths of metallic trim. Position a length of trim approximately ¼" (6mm) in from each long edge on the right side of the straps. Stitch in place with a zigzag stitch (page 17).

2" (5cm)

FIGURE 5

7. *attach the straps*

Pin the straps, right side facing out, 4" (10cm) in from the side seams and with the raw ends of the straps 2" (5cm) down from the upper edge of the bag. Topstitch each end in place, stitching over the existing topstitching along the strap's edges. Topstitch another line about 2" (5cm) long down the center of the strap. (FIGURE 5)

COVER THE RAW ENDS OF THE STRAPS: Cut four 2" (5cm) lengths of trim. Place one length over each strap end, covering the raw edge. Zigzag stitch the trim in place. (FIGURE 5, INSET)

first time's a *charm cardi*

Confession time: Until I designed this *cardigan*, I had never sewn with knits. I was afraid of them. I thought I needed *something special*, like a special sewing machine or special thread or some magical special ability to *sew stretchy things*. Turns out, I was completely wrong! Sewing knits is very similar to sewing woven fabrics, and you use all the *same techniques* and tools. So even if you've never sewn with knits, give this cardi a try—you'll be glad you did.

finished dimensions
WIDTH: Sized to fit your body
LENGTH: 28" (71cm)

supplies
* Basic sewing supplies (page 11)
* Approximately 2 yards (1.8m) stretch knit fabric (see Note)

note
This garment is sized to fit your measurements so the exact amount of fabric needed will vary. Read the entire pattern and take your body measurements (Step 1) to determine the exact amount you'll need. Buy extra when in doubt.

1. measure + cut
BACK: Measure your bust circumference and divide that number in half. Add 3" (7.5cm) for measurement **A**. Cut a rectangle with a width of measurement **A** and a length of 29" (74cm).

FRONTS: Cut 2 rectangles with a width equal to half of measurement **A** minus 4" (10cm) and a length of 29" (74cm). **(FIGURE 1)**

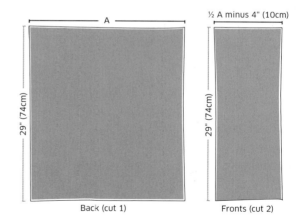

Back (cut 1)   Fronts (cut 2)

FIGURE 1

SLEEVES: Cut 2 rectangles 24" (61cm) wide and 11" (28cm) long. (This creates a very wide, kimono-style elbow-length sleeve. If you prefer a different-sized sleeve, adjust the length and width accordingly here. Wrap a tape measure loosely around your upper arm to help determine the sleeve width you prefer.)

FRONT FACING: You will also need to cut two 7" (18cm) strips for the front facing, but you must first construct the cardigan fronts and back to determine the necessary measurement. Be sure to allow for these extra pieces when cutting. (See Step 7 for more details.) **(FIGURE 2)**

2. sew the shoulder seams

With right sides together, pin the fronts to the back at the top edges (there will be a gap between the front pieces, as shown). Sew each front to the back across the top edge with a ½" (13mm) seam allowance. **(FIGURE 3)**

3. attach the sleeves

Open the front and back piece and lay it flat, right side up. With right sides together, pin one sleeve to the cardigan front and back, centering the wide end of the sleeve over the shoulder seam, with the edges aligned. Sew with a ½" (13mm) seam allowance. **(FIGURE 4)** Press the seam allowance *toward* the sleeve (this is important for creating a nice underarm seam in Step 5). Repeat for the remaining sleeve.

4. shape the neck back

With wrong sides together, fold the cardigan back in half vertically and mark the center point (on the right side) at the top edge with a pin; unfold and lay flat, right side up. Using a

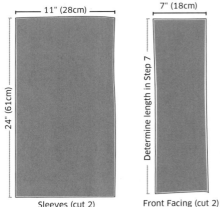

11" (28cm)   7" (18cm)

24" (61cm)   Determine length in Step 7

Sleeves (cut 2)   Front Facing (cut 2)

FIGURE 2

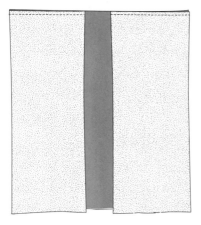

FIGURE 3

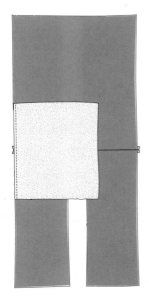

FIGURE 4

small plate or other round object, trace a curve onto the back, centered between the 2 front pieces, about 1" (2.5cm) deep. Cut the marked curve out of the neckline. (FIGURE 5)

5. *sew the side and underarm seams*

With right sides together, fold the cardigan at the shoulder seams and align the underarm and side edges; pin. Beginning at the bottom (hem edge), sew along the side and underarm seams with a ½" (13mm) seam allowance. (FIGURE 6)

6. *hem the bottom edge*

NOTE: It may seem counterintuitive to hem the bottom edge before the front facing has been added, but the facing will be finished separately in Step 7.

Turn the bottom hem under ½" (13mm) and press. Turn the hem under again 1" (2.5cm); press, then pin. Topstitch (page 17) the hem in place. If your fabric is very lightweight, add a strip of lightweight interfacing (page 19) to the hem allowance before you sew it in place to stabilize the stitching.

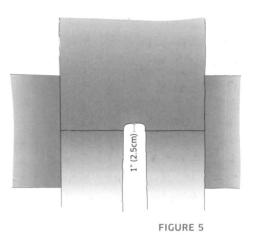

1" (2.5cm)

FIGURE 5

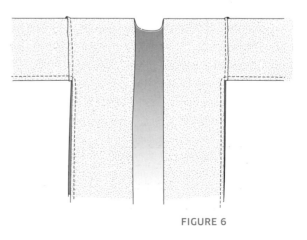

FIGURE 6

7. make the front facing

With a tape measure, measure from the bottom hem along the front edge and around the neckline to the center back. (FIGURE 7) Cut 2 strips of fabric this length plus 1" (2.5cm), and 7" (18cm) wide. With right sides together and the 7" (18cm) ends aligned, sew the 2 strips together with a ½" (13mm) seam allowance. Press the seam allowance open. With right sides together and long edges aligned, fold the strip in half lengthwise; pin then sew the 2 short ends closed with a ½" (13mm) seam allowance. (FIGURE 8) Trim the corners (page 19) and turn the strip right side out. Press.

8. attach the facing

With right sides together and raw edges aligned, pin the facing in place along the cardigan's fronts and (back) neck. Align the facing's center seam with the cardigan's center back. Sew in place, using a ½" (13mm) seam allowance and sewing through both layers of the facing and the cardigan body. Begin sewing at the bottom and work up one front side to the center back, then stop, backstitch (page 17), and clip the thread. Start sewing again at the bottom of the other side of the front, sewing up the front to the center back. (Working up from each bottom edge ensures that the finished bottom edges of the facing will be perfectly aligned with the hem.) (FIGURE 9)

Press the seam allowance toward the cardigan body and, on the right side, topstitch in place.

FIGURE 7

FIGURE 8

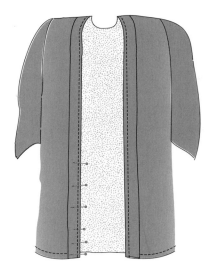

FIGURE 9

9. hem the sleeves

Turn the raw edge of the sleeve under ½"
(13mm) and press. Turn under another 1"
(2.5cm); press, then pin. Topstitch the hem
in place.

GET KNITTY WITH IT

I admit, I was a knit newbie before making this
cardigan. But sewing with knits is easier than you'd
think! Here are a few pointers I learned along
the way.

* Because knits stretch, they tend to shift as you're
  cutting them, which makes the cutting slow going.
  But just take your time and you'll get through it. I
  find it easier to use a rotary cutter, straightedge,
  and cutting mat.
* Pin your pieces well before sewing to discourage
  the fabric from shifting mid-seam.
* Stretch the fabric *slightly* as you sew it. If you
  stretch it too much, it will distort the seam.
* Knits don't unravel, so if you want to keep things
  really simple, you don't have to bother finishing
  your raw edges on hems, sleeves, etc.
* Steam-press each seam after you sew it. Otherwise you'll get discouraged and think you've
  sewn an ugly, distorted seam. Stitching tends to
  bunch up on knits, but a quick press with the iron
  smoothes it right out. All better.

heavy metal *bag*

I love to sew things that look like they couldn't possibly be *handmade*—and this *bag* fits that bill to a T. Faux ostrich is a luxe departure from a traditional fabric choice, and metal hardware lends a ***professional touch***. These materials are a fun challenge to work with, but if you prefer, you can also use this pattern to sew a bag from a woven fabric. For a softer look, choose round studs rather than the pointed ones I used.

finished dimensions
WIDTH: 15" (38cm)
LENGTH: (excluding strap): 15" (38cm)

supplies
* Basic sewing supplies (page 11)
* 1 yard (91cm) lightweight vinyl faux leather
* ½ yard (46cm) medium-weight cotton (for lining)
* ¼ yard (23cm) medium-weight muslin (for stabilizer)
* Four ¾" (2cm) nailheads/studs
* Four ¼" (6mm) nailheads/studs
* Four 1⅞" (4.8cm) metal rings
* Low-tack masking tape
* Tissue paper
* Clapper or hardcover book
* Heavy-duty sewing machine needle

fabric suggestions
I used lightweight faux leather vinyl for this project. If you prefer, you can make this bag with a traditional woven fabric; medium- to heavyweight cottons and blends would work great here.

notes

1. Be sure to read the Working with Vinyl sidebar (page 62) before beginning this project.
2. If you use a woven fabric instead of vinyl, simply use standard ironing and sewing methods.

1. *measure + cut*

BAG BODY AND LINING: Cut two 23" x 12" (58.5cm x 30.5cm) pieces from the exterior fabric and 2 the same size from the lining fabric. Cut a 2" (5cm) square from each bottom corner.

FACING: Cut two 15" x 4" (38cm x 10cm) pieces from the exterior fabric, and 2 the same size from the muslin (the stabilizer).

SIDE STRAPS: Cut two 8" x 4" (20.5cm x 10cm) pieces from the exterior fabric.

SHOULDER STRAP: Cut one 20" x 4" (51cm x 10cm) piece from the exterior fabric. **(FIGURE 1)**

2. *make the pleats*

Mark pleat placement on the top edge of each bag body piece as follows: Starting at the left edge, measure a point 5" (12.5cm) from the edge. Mark this as point **A**. Measure over 2" (5cm) from point **A**, and mark point **B**. Mark point **C** 2" (5cm) from point **B**. Mark point **D** 5" (12.5cm) from point **C**. Mark point **E** 2" (5cm) from point **D**. Mark point **F** 2" (5cm) from point **E**. **(FIGURE 1)**

Fold points **A** and **C** to meet at point **B**. Fold points **D** and **F** to meet at point **E**. Pin in place. (If using vinyl, be sure to place pins *only* in the seam allowance.) Press as described in the Working with Vinyl sidebar (page 62).

3. *add stabilizer to the facing*

NOTE: For added strength, a stabilizing layer of muslin is sewn to the wrong side of the facing.

With wrong sides together, sew one piece of muslin facing to each bag facing, sewing around all 4 sides with a ¼" (6mm) seam allowance.

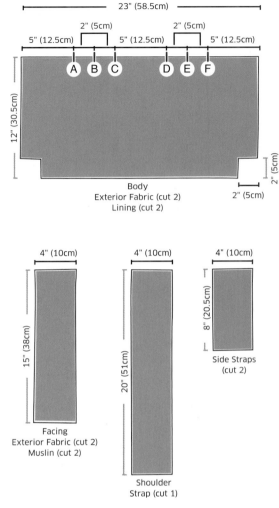

Body
Exterior Fabric (cut 2)
Lining (cut 2)

Facing
Exterior Fabric (cut 2)
Muslin (cut 2)

Shoulder
Strap (cut 1)

Side Straps
(cut 2)

FIGURE 1

FIGURE 2

straight-up chic fashion

4. attach the facing to the bag sides

With right sides together, pin then sew one facing piece to each bag body piece along the pleated edge, with a ½" (13mm) seam allowance. Press the seam allowance toward the facing.

Topstitch (page 17) on the facing close to the folded edge (see Working with Vinyl sidebar for tips on topstitching vinyl), placing a piece of tissue paper on top of the facing before sewing. Tear the tissue away after completing the topstitching. (You may need to carefully remove any small pieces of tissue with tweezers.) (FIGURE 2)

5. assemble the bag body

With right sides together, sew the bag body pieces together along the side seams with a ½" (13mm) seam allowance. Press the seam allowances open. Sew the bottom seam with a ½" (13mm) seam allowance. (It will be hard to press this seam with an iron, so it's not necessary to do so.) (FIGURE 3)

Fold the bag so that the right sides of the bottom and side seams meet at the bottom corners. Sew each corner opening closed with a ½" (13mm) seam allowance. (FIGURE 3 INSETS)

Turn the bag right side out. Press the corner seams on the fold.

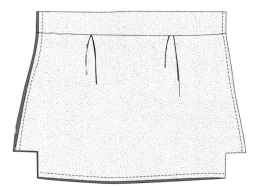

FIGURE 3

6. make the side straps

Using the strap pieces cut in Step 1, make 2 side straps following the directions on page 20.

Sandwich the folded strap between two 1"- (2.5cm-) wide strips of tissue paper. Topstitch the strap through the tissue paper close to the folded edge along both long edges. Tear the tissue paper away after completing the stitching.

Insert the strap through 2 of the metal rings as shown in **FIGURE 4**. Bring the short ends of the strap to meet so that strap forms a ring. With ends butted together (not overlapping), whipstitch (page 15) the ends together. (If you're making your bag from fabric rather than vinyl, zigzag stitch the ends of the strap to prevent the raw edges from fraying.) Flatten the strap so that the whipstitched seam is at the center back of the strap, and a ring is on each end. Repeat for the remaining strap.

7. attach the side straps

Position an assembled side strap over each side seam of the bag body, with the folded top end of each strap ¾" (2cm) down from the raw edge of the bag facing. Hold the straps in place temporarily by taping the rings and the ends of the straps down with low-tack masking tape.

Place a 1"- (2.5cm-) wide strip of tissue paper over each side strap, and topstitch them in place as follows: Stitching close to the strap edge and pivoting at the corners, sew down one side of the strap, across the strap, up the other edge, and back across to form a rectangle of stitching that is approximately 1" (2.5cm) long and centered on the strap, as shown in **FIGURE 5**.

FIGURE 4

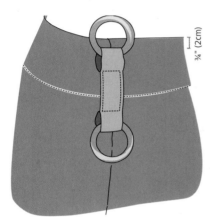

¾" (2cm)

FIGURE 5

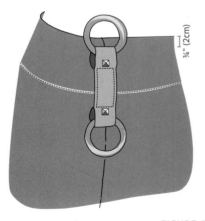

¾" (2cm)

FIGURE 6

8. install the studs

Refer to **FIGURE 6** for placement. Mark placement for a ¼" (16mm) stud near each end of each side strap, centered between the ring and the topstitching. With an awl or seam ripper, carefully pierce the side strap through all layers at each mark. Following the manufacturer's directions for installing studs, insert a stud through each hole.

9. sew the lining

Mark and sew pleats on the lining pieces exactly as you did for the bag body in Step 2.

Place both lining pieces right sides together; pin. Sew the side seams with a ½" (13mm) seam allowance, leaving a 6" (15cm) opening at the center of one side seam. (It's important to sew the top and bottom of the side seam and leave the opening in the center; otherwise finishing will be tricky.) Press the seam allowances open.

Sew the bottom seam with a ½" (13mm) seam allowance and press the seam allowance open. Sew the corners as you did for the bag exterior in Step 5. **(FIGURE 3, INSET)**

10. attach the lining to the bag

Turn the lining inside out and place the bag exterior inside the lining with right sides together, aligning the top raw edges and side seams. (Be sure to fold the side straps out of the way.) Sew the facing and lining together at the top raw edge with a ½" (13mm) seam allowance. To turn the bag right side out, pull the lining up over bag, gently working the bag exterior body through the opening on the side seam of the lining. From the right side of the fabric, press the seam allowance toward the lining. Whipstitch the opening in the lining closed, and turn the lining to the interior of bag. (**NOTE:** When the lining is folded to the inside, the facing will also fold to the inside of the bag, for a slouchy look. You do not need to press or stitch the facing at the fold, but rather let it slouch in naturally.)

11. make the shoulder strap

Using the piece cut in Step 1, make the shoulder strap following the directions on page 20.

12. attach the shoulder strap

Feed 2" (5cm) of the shoulder strap through each of the upper rings on the 2 side straps. Fold the strap back on itself around the ring and topstitch this 2" (5cm) overlap in place with a rectangle as you did for the side straps in Step 7, sandwiching the strap between 2 layers of tissue paper before stitching.

13. install the studs

Referring to the photograph (above), mark placement for two ¾" (2cm) studs above the rings on each overlapped end of the shoulder strap. Install studs as you did for the side straps in Step 8.

straight-up chic fashion

sewing school *skirt*

I like to think of this skirt as a little sewing school all wrapped up in a single project. You'll learn to make pleats, a *fitted waistband*, button plackets, and buttonholes—all while sewing straight lines only. And even better, at the end of this lesson, you'll have an adorably *preppy-chic* skirt to show off. (I love it with flats or boots!)

finished dimensions
WIDTH: Sized to fit your body
LENGTH: 20¾" (51cm)

supplies
* Basic sewing supplies (page 11)
* Approximately 2 yards (1.8m) fabric (see Note)
* ½ yard (46cm) lightweight fusible interfacing
* Five 1⅛"- (2.8cm-) diameter buttons
* All-purpose thread to match your fabric
* All-purpose thread to contrast with your fabric

fabric suggestions
A medium to heavyweight woven is ideal for this skirt. I used a cotton twill, but light denim, corduroy, or wool would all work great, too.

note

This garment is sized to fit your measurements so the exact amount of fabric needed will vary. Read the entire pattern and take your body measurements (Step 1) to determine the exact amount you'll need. Buy extra when in doubt.

1. *measure + cut*

SKIRT FRONTS: Measure your waist circumference and add 1½" (3.8cm) ease for measurement A. Divide A by 4 and add 13¼" (33.5cm) for measurement B. Cut 2 rectangles with a width of B and a length of 22¾" (58cm).

SKIRT BACK: Divide A by 2 and add 10" (25.5cm) for measurement C. Cut one rectangle with a width of C and a length of 22¾" (58cm). (FIGURE 1)

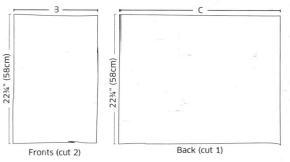

Fronts (cut 2)   Back (cut 1)

FIGURE 1

INTERFACING: Cut two 10" x 22¾" (25.5cm x 58cm) pieces of fusible interfacing for the skirt front. You will also need to cut interfacing for the waistband; measurements to be determined in Step 9.

WAISTBAND: You will need to cut fabric for a waistband, but you can't do this until you've determined the size you'll need in Step 9. Be sure to reserve enough fabric to cut two pieces which are 2¾" (7cm) wide by at least your waist measurement plus 1" (2.5cm). **(FIGURE 2)**

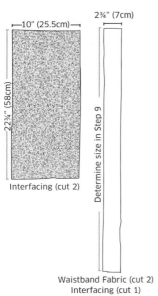

Interfacing (cut 2)

Waistband Fabric (cut 2)
Interfacing (cut 1)

FIGURE 2

2. *fuse interfacing to skirt fronts*

Fuse one piece of interfacing (page 19) to the wrong side of each skirt front, along one 22¾" (58cm) edge. The interfaced edges will be the center front and the noninterfaced edges will be the side seams, so make sure you fuse opposite edges on each skirt front piece. **(FIGURE 3)**

3. *mark the pleats*

This skirt has 1½"- (3.8cm-) deep knife pleats that face away from the skirt center. Be sure to refer to the illustrations for clarification in marking the skirt front and back pieces for pleat placement.

MARK FRONT PLEATS: Lay each skirt front piece with the right side facing up. Work at the top edge of each skirt front: Mark point **A** 9½" (24cm) from the interfaced edge. Mark point **B** 3" (7.5cm) from point **A**. Mark point **C** 1½" (3.8cm) from point **B**. Mark point **D** 3" (7.5cm) from point **C**. **(FIGURE 4)**

MARK BACK PLEATS: Fold the skirt back in half to find the center back; mark. Open the back and lay it flat, right side facing up. Referring

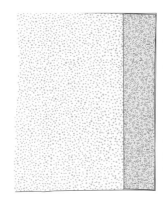

FIGURE 3

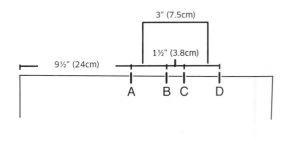

Right Front

FIGURE 4

to the measurements in **FIGURE 5**, mark the top edge of the skirt back for pleat placement (A–F) as you did for the fronts. Be sure to mark points A–F on *both* the left and the right sides of the center back.

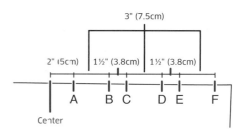

Back

FIGURE 5

4. make the pleats

FOLD FRONT PLEATS: Fold the fabric *away* from the interfaced edge so that point A meets B and point C meets D; pin. (**FIGURE 6**) This will result in two 1½"- (3.8cm-) deep pleats, each folded in a Z shape, facing *away* from the skirt center. (The pleats on the right skirt front will be folded to the right, and the pleats on the left skirt front will be folded to the left.)

FOLD BACK PLEATS: Fold the pleats on each side of the back *toward* the side seams so that point A meets B, point C meets D, and point E meets F. This will result in three 1½"- (3.8cm-) deep pleats on each side of the back, for 6 pleats total. (**FIGURE 7**)

FRONT AND BACK: Press the pleats and baste along their top edges with a ¼" (6mm) seam allowance.

5. sew skirt fronts to back

With right sides together, pin the skirt back to each skirt front piece along the noninterfaced 22¾" (58cm) edges (side seams), aligning raw edges. Sew with a ¼" (6mm) French seam (page 18).

6. press facing and hem guide lines

NOTE: In this step, you will fold and press the skirt's facing and hem to create guidelines that will be used in Steps 7 and 8.

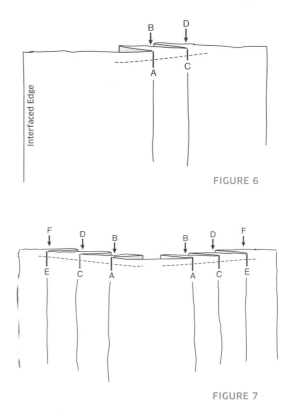

FIGURE 6

FIGURE 7

On both skirt fronts, turn the interfaced edge under 2½" (6.5cm) and press. Turn it under another 2½" (6.5cm) and press. Turn under the hem ½" (13mm) along the bottom of the front and back pieces and press. Turn under the hem another 2" (5cm) and press.

Unfold to proceed, using the pressed lines as guidelines for Steps 7 and 8.

7. *fold and sew the facing*

On one skirt front, with right sides together, fold the facing edge to the front 5" (12.5cm) along the pressed guideline you made in Step 6. Keeping this fold in place, fold the raw edge back to meet the fold line (the fabric will be folded in a 2½"- [6.5cm-] wide Z); pin. Sew across the facing along the hemline (the pressed guideline 2½" [6.5cm] above the bottom raw edge). **(FIGURE 8)** Repeat for the remaining skirt front.

Trim the outside corners as shown and turn the facings to the wrong side. Sew 2 lines of topstitching (page 17) on both facings along both long folded edges. These are your button plackets.

8. *hem the skirt*

Repress the hem allowance along the folds made in Step 6 and topstitch it in place close to the hem allowance's top edge.

9. *make the waistband*

Measure the skirt's entire top edge and add 1" (2.5cm). Cut 2 waistband fabric pieces and one interfacing piece this length by 2¾" (7cm) wide. Fuse the interfacing to the wrong side of one waistband piece.

SEW THE FIRST WAISTBAND PIECE: With right sides together, pin the interfaced rectangle to

tip

Show off your favorite big buttons on this garment—but don't go larger than 1⅛" (2.8cm), or the button will be too large to fit on the waistband.

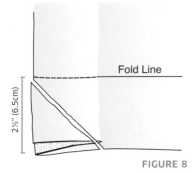

2½" (6.5cm)

Fold Line

FIGURE 8

the skirt with the long edges aligned and short ends extending ½" (13mm) past the skirt facing edges. Sew in place with a ½" (13mm) seam allowance. (FIGURE 9) Press the seam open, with the seam allowance pressed toward the waistband.

SEW THE SECOND WAISTBAND PIECE: Fold under one long edge of the remaining waistband piece ½" (13mm) and press. With right sides together and raw edges aligned, pin this piece to the waistband piece already sewn to the skirt, aligning the long folded edge with the waistband seam. Sew around the ends and top edge with a ½" (13mm) seam allowance. (FIGURE 10)

Trim the corners (page 19) and turn the facing right side out. Use a pointy tool to gently poke out the corners. (FIGURE 11) The waistband will now be finished on 3 sides, with the folded edge on the interior. Pin the folded edge to the inside and whipstitch (page 15) to secure.

10. *add buttonholes and buttons*

(Refer to your sewing machine's manual for instructions on making buttonholes.) On the right skirt front, make a 1¼"- (3cm-) long horizontal buttonhole centered on the waistband and starting 1" (2.5cm) from the edge. Add 4 vertical buttonholes down the length of the right skirt front button placket 1⅛" (2.8cm) from the edge and spaced 2½" (6.5cm) apart. (FIGURE 12)

Use a seam ripper to open all buttonholes. Close the skirt front with the buttonhole placket laying over the left skirt front. Make a button placement mark through each buttonhole onto the left skirt front. Sew a button on each mark.

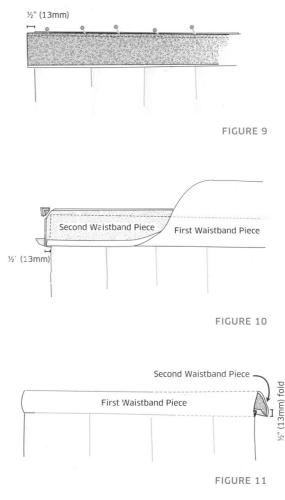

½" (13mm)

FIGURE 9

Second Waistband Piece   First Waistband Piece

½" (13mm)

FIGURE 10

Second Waistband Piece

First Waistband Piece

½" (13mm) fold

FIGURE 11

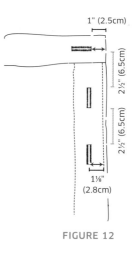

1" (2.5cm)

2½" (6.5cm)

2½" (6.5cm)

1⅛" (2.8cm)

FIGURE 12

origami *dress*

Now that you're getting comfortable sewing straight lines, are you ready for a little challenge? Take it up a notch with this swingy dress, featuring a ***fancy folded trim*** that looks like it's straight out of a designer boutique. This pattern will also show you how to install a zipper, using ***my favorite*** easy method. What's more, multiple colors of fabric trick the eye into thinking this design is even more complex than it is. All in all, this dress packs ***major punch***, using only basic skills. Go for it!

finished dimensions
WIDTH: Sized to fit your body
LENGTH: 31" (79cm)

supplies
* Basic sewing supplies (page 11)
* Approximately 2 yards (1.8m) main color fabric (light purple) (see Note)
* ¼ yard (23cm) accent-color fabric (gray)
* ½ yard (46cm) contrasting-color fabric (dark purple)
* 11" (28cm) standard zipper
* Hook and eye
* All-purpose thread to contrast with fabric

fabric suggestions
For the body of this dress I recommend a lightweight cotton or cotton blend. Medium-weight cottons don't drape as well.

note

This garment is sized to fit your measurements so the exact amount of fabric needed will vary. Read the entire pattern and take your body measurements (Step 1) to determine the exact amount you'll need. Buy extra when in doubt.

1. ***measure + cut***

   DRESS FRONT AND BACK: Measure your body's circumference just above the bust for measurement A. From your main fabric (light purple), cut 2 rectangles with a width equal to A and a length of 31" (79cm). **(FIGURE 1)**

Front/Back (cut 2)

FIGURE 1

CHEST BANDS: Divide measurement **A** in half and add 1" (2.5cm) for measurement **B**. From the accent (gray) fabric, cut 4 rectangles with a length of **B** and a width of 2½" (6.5cm).

ORIGAMI TRIM: From the accent (gray) fabric, cut 3 rectangles that are 3½" (9cm) wide and as long as measurement **A** plus 12" (30cm).

STRAPS: From the contrasting fabric (dark purple), cut 2 rectangles 2" (5cm) wide by 18" (45.5cm) long. **(FIGURE 2)**

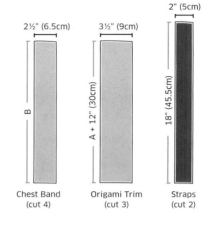

FIGURE 2

2. *gather the front and back*

Gather the top edge of the dress body pieces as follows: Baste (page 17) the top edge of the dress body front and back ¼" (6mm) from raw edge. Pull the bobbin thread to gather each piece of fabric down to a width of measurement **B**. Distribute the gathers evenly. **(FIGURE 3)**

3. *attach the chest bands*

With right sides together, pin then sew a chest band piece along the gathered edge of the front and back pieces with a ½" (13mm) seam allowance **(FIGURE 3)**. Trim the seam allowance from the dress body piece (not the band) and press the seam allowance toward the chest band.

FIGURE 3

4. *mark the center point*

With wrong sides together, fold each front and back piece in half vertically to find the center points. Mark these points on the chest band with a pin or marking tool. (These points will be needed in Step 7 to position the straps.)

5. *sew the right-hand side seam*

With right sides together, pin then sew the front and back together along the right-hand side edge with a ½" (13mm) seam allowance. (You will sew the left-hand side seam in Step 10.) Press the seam allowance open.

6. make the straps

Using the pieces you cut in Step 1, make 2 straps following the directions on page 20.

7. attach the straps

With right sides together, pin one end of each strap to the chest band 4½" (11.5cm) from the center point of the dress front. (There will be a total of 9" [23cm] between straps.) Pin the other ends of the straps to the back chest band, as you did on the front. **(FIGURE 4)**

Try on the dress to check the strap placement and length, adjusting as needed. With right sides together and raw edges aligned, sew each strap to the front and back chest band, using a ¼" (6mm) seam allowance.

8. assemble the facing

With wrong sides together, and with a ½" (13mm) seam allowance, pin then sew the 2 remaining chest band pieces together along one short end to make the facing. Press the seam allowance open. Fold one long edge under ½" (13mm) and press.

9. attach the facing

With right sides together and side seams aligned, pin the facing's *unpressed* long edge along the top edge of chest band. Sew along the top edge with a ½" (13mm) seam allowance. Press the seam allowance toward the facing.

tip

You can turn this dress into a special-occasion affair just by upgrading the details. Use a slinky black fabric for the body, and consider stitching a bead or rhinestone onto the center of each diamond in the trim. Ooh la la!

4½" (11.5cm)

FIGURE 4

73

origami dress

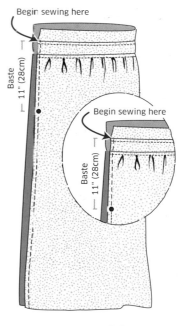

Begin sewing here

Baste 11" (28cm)

Begin sewing here

Baste 11" (28cm)

FIGURE 5

10. *sew the left-hand side seam*

With right sides together and raw edges aligned, pin the remaining side seam together. Beginning at the (top) facing seam (*not* at the top raw edge), baste the seam for 11" (28cm) with a ½" (13mm) seam allowance. After basting for 11" (28cm), change your machine's stitch length to a regular stitch, backstitch to reinforce, and sew the remainder of the side seam with a regular stitch. Press the seam allowance open. **(FIGURE 5)**

11. *install the zipper*

(Refer to the Don't Fear the Zipper sidebar on page 86.) With the dress wrong side out and with the right side of the zipper facing the fabric, pin the zipper over the basted section of the left side seam, centering the teeth over the basted seam. **(FIGURE 6)**

Attach a zipper foot to your machine. Starting at the top of the zipper, sew down one side of the zipper. When you reach the bottom, pivot and sew across the zipper, then pivot to sew up the other side of the zipper, stopping when you reach the top. **(FIGURE 7)**

Working on the right side of the dress, use a seam ripper to gently remove the basting stitches from the seam and expose the zipper.

12. *make the origami strip*

With right sides together and short ends aligned, sew the 3 trim strips together with a ¼" (6mm) seam allowance to make one long strip. Press the seam allowances open.

SEW THE STRIP: Fold the strip in half lengthwise with right sides together and long edges aligned; pin. Sew the long edge with a ¼" (6mm) seam allowance. Turn the strip right side out, center the seam on the strip, and

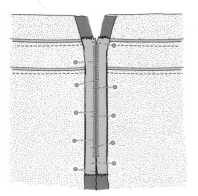

FIGURE 6

FIGURE 7

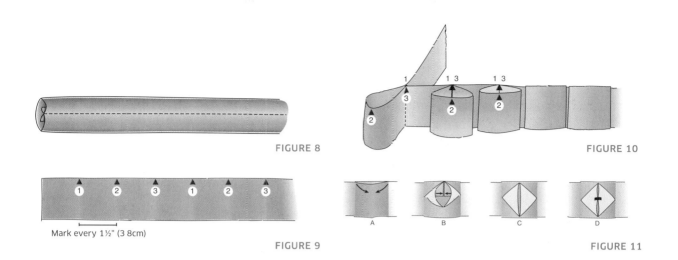

FIGURE 8

FIGURE 10

Mark every 1½" (3 8cm)

FIGURE 9

FIGURE 11

press. (The side with the seam is the wrong side of the strip.) (FIGURE 8)

Beginning 2" (6cm) from the edge mark the strip every 1½" (3.8cm) on the right side of the strip. (FIGURE 9)

Fold the strip with *wrong* sides together so that every third mark meets; pin. Sew the strip at each meeting point, creating a series of loops on the strip. Press each loop flat. (FIGURE 10)

FOLD EACH LOOP INTO A DIAMOND SHAPE, ORIGAMI STYLE: Refer to FIGURE 11. NOTE: You can view a video of this technique on my website: www.brettbara.com.

A. On one flattened loop, pull the top front edge of the folded loop open.

B. Bring the two side edges of the loop together to meet in the center, forming a diamond shape.

C. Press flat.

D. With contrasting thread, secure each diamond in place in its center, either by hand or machine. To secure by machine, set your stitch for a wide, short zigzag. Make several zigzag stitches in the center of the diamond, backstitching a few times to reinforce.

Fold the next diamond in the same manner, except open the loop from the bottom edge. Fold and stitch all the diamond shapes on the strip, alternating folding from the top and the bottom edges.

ATTACH THE ORIGAMI STRIP TO THE DRESS: Fold under the raw edges of the strip and pin the *wrong* side of the finished origami strip over the right side of the chest band; trim the length of the strip if necessary. Whipstitch (page 15) the strip to the *band* along both long edges.

13. finish the facing

Fold the facing to the inside. Turn under the facing's raw side edges and whipstitch them in place. Whipstitch the long folded edge of the facing in place.

14. hem

Turn under the hem ½" (13mm) and press. Turn it under again 1" (2.5cm) and press. Topstitch (page 17) the hem in place.

15. attach the hook and eye

Hand-sew the hook and eye to the wrong side of the band, above the zipper, following the directions on the package.

cozy, crafty
home

Nothing makes me feel more *at home* in my space than surrounding myself with things I've made. A few handmade touches are all it takes to make your nest divine.

Will you believe me when I tell you that you don't have to be an expert sewer to make it happen? That's right—beautiful, handmade *decor is* as *easy* as a few straight seams.

If you've got a ho-hum room that needs some flair, the quickest and easiest way to bring it to life is to sew a few accessories. If you're a beginner, I recommend starting with *Customized Curtains*, Two Ways, for a look at two great basic curtain styles. Or try your hand at the World's Easiest Zippered Throw Pillow—you won't believe how easy it is to install a zipper using my method. And for a *super-quick* dose of *diy decor*, don't miss the 15-Minute Shams.

With a few *simple skills* under your belt, you can try the Clutter-Busting Bucket Tote to corral clutter, the Make-It-Your-Way Ottoman Cover to learn the basics of making slipcovers, or the DIY Duvet Cover to add some *flair* to your bed. To me, a quilt is the ultimate in homey style, and this chapter will walk you through the steps of sewing a patchwork masterpiece. Quilting may seem challenging, but you can make *amazing quilts* using only basic skills by choosing bold but simple designs, like the Pixelated Throw and the Wonky Diamonds On Point quilt. (The latter is not for the faint of heart, but the stunning results are worth the effort!)

Everything in this chapter is designed to be a statement piece, and you can personalize each project by customizing it with your fabric choices. Create a *bold look* by choosing a loud print, or go quieter with a range of coordinating solids. Try taking a risk and breaking out of matchy-matchy mode, by mixing groups of fabrics with similar color palettes or themes.

So don't be afraid to *experiment* and *try new looks* with your decor. That's the beauty of knowing how to make it yourself!

customized curtains, *two ways*

Need to wake up a boring room? It's easy—whip up some curtains! Even complete *beginners* can tackle this project; these drapes take only an afternoon to sew and they truly *transform* a house into a *home*. In this pattern, I'll show you how to make two types of curtains: a basic curtain panel with a ball-fringe trim and a lined tab curtain, both of which can be made to fit any window. Add a fabric you love, and you'll have custom decor *in a flash*.

finished dimensions
Sized to fit your window of choice

supplies

* Basic sewing supplies (page 11)
* Curtain rod
* **For basic curtain panel with ball fringe:**

  Fabric of your choice (determine the amount you'll need in Step 1, page 80)

  Length of ball fringe sufficient to cover the width of your curtain panels
* **For lined tab curtain panel:**

  Fabric of your choice (determine the amount you'll need in Step 1, page 82)

  Lining fabric (determine the amount you'll need in Step 1)

note

This pattern makes a rod pocket that fits a slim curtain rod (such as a tension rod). If you are using a thicker curtain rod, you may need to make a deeper pocket. Measure the diameter of your rod, and add that extra length to your fabric.

curtain panel with ball fringe

1. measure + cut

CURTAIN PANEL: Measure the width of your window (A). (If your curtain rod hangs outside the window, measure from the ends of the curtain rod.) Next, measure the distance from the curtain rod to the point where you'd like the bottom of the curtain to hang (B).

Determine how gathered you would like your curtain to be (C). (For a typical amount of gathering, double measurement A.)

Add 4" (10cm) to measurement C; this is the width you will need to cut your fabric.

Add 10½" (26.5cm) to measurement B; this is the length you will need to cut your fabric.

Cut your fabric to the above dimensions (see Cutting Large Fabric Pieces sidebar on page 25).

2. hem the bottom edge

Turn under the bottom edge of the curtain 4" (10cm) and press. (FIGURE 1) Turn up another 4" (10cm) and press again. (FIGURE 2) Topstitch (page 17) close to the upper folded edge. (FIGURE 3)

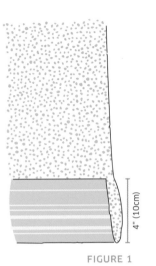

FIGURE 1

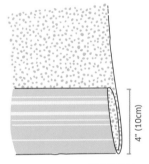

FIGURE 2

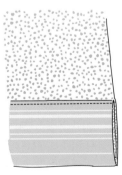

FIGURE 3

3. hem the sides

Turn under one side edge 1" (2.5cm) and press. (FIGURE 4) Turn it under another 1" (2.5cm) and press. (FIGURE 5) Topstitch close to the inner folded edge. (FIGURE 6) Repeat for the remaining side of the curtain.

4. make the pocket for the curtain rod

Turn under the remaining (top) raw edge ½" (13mm) and press. Turn it under another 2" (5cm) and press again. Topstitch close to the inner folded edge. (FIGURE 7)

5. attach trim

Pin the ball fringe along the hemmed edge of the curtain, turning under its raw edge ½" (13mm). Sew it in place using a zigzag stitch (page 17) and thread to match the trim.

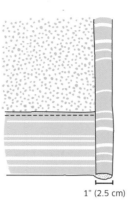

1" (2.5 cm)

FIGURE 4

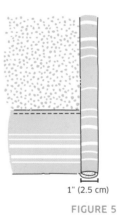

1" (2.5 cm)

FIGURE 5

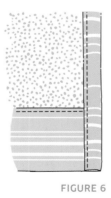

FIGURE 6

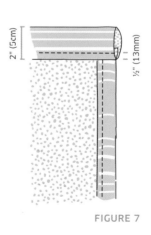

2" (5cm)   ½" (13mm)

FIGURE 7

lined tab curtain

1. measure + cut

CURTAIN PANEL AND LINING: Measure following the directions in Step 1 on page 80 for measurements **A**, **B**, and **C**.

Add 1" (2.5cm) to measurement **C** to determine the width you will need to cut your fabric.

Add 8½" (21.5cm) to measurement **B** to determine the length you will need to cut your fabric.

Cut one panel to these dimensions from your curtain fabric, and another panel the same size from your lining fabric.

FOR THE TABS: Determine how many tabs, spaced 10-12" (25.5-30.5cm) apart, will fit on your curtain panel. Cut this number of 9" x 6" (23cm x 15cm) tab pieces from your curtain fabric.

2. sew the tabs

Fold each tab piece in half lengthwise with right sides together, aligning the 9" (23cm) edges; pin in place. Sew along the raw 9" (23cm) edges using a ½" (13mm) seam allowance. (FIGURE 8)

Turn the tab right side out and press. Repeat to make all the tabs.

FIGURE 8

3. hem the bottom edges

Hem the bottom edges of the curtain and lining piece, following Step 2 on page 80.

4. assemble the tabs, lining, and front

Place the lining on the floor or work surface with the right side facing up. Fold the tabs in half with short ends together, then position them on the top edge of the lining, spaced evenly apart, aligning the raw ends of the tabs with the raw edge of the lining. Place the curtain panel, right side down, on top of the tabs and lining, sandwiching the tabs between the curtain panel and the lining, aligning the raw edge of the curtain panel with the raw edges of the lining and tabs. (FIGURE 9) Pin all the layers together, but leave the hemmed edges (bottom) unpinned. Make sure all raw edges are perfectly aligned so the curtain will hang straight. Using a ½" (13mm) seam allowance, sew all the layers together around 3 sides, leaving the hemmed edges open.

Trim the seam allowance at the corners (page 19) and turn right side out. Use a pointy tool to gently poke out the corners. Press. Topstitch around 3 sides (again leaving the hemmed edge open), stitching close to the edge. (FIGURE 10)

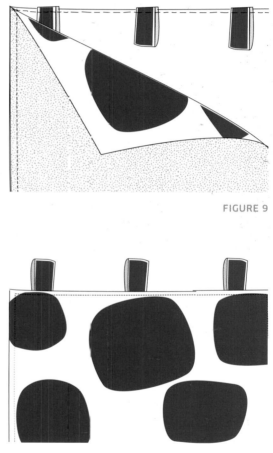

FIGURE 9

FIGURE 10

world's easiest zippered *throw pillow*

If you have a fear of *installing zippers*, this project is for you.
Give it a try, and I promise you'll soon be sewing a zipper into
everything in sight! *In fact*, this pillow cover is so easy to make,
you might find yourself re-covering your *throw pillows* every
season, or every time you find yourself in the mood for a little
decor change. It's really that *easy*!

supplies

* Basic sewing supplies (page 11)
* Approximately 1 yard (91cm) fabric of your choice (see Step 1 to determine the exact amount of fabric you'll need)
* Zipper, 4" (10cm) shorter than the width of your pillow
* Pillow form, desired size

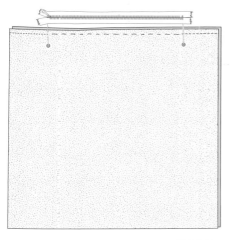

FIGURE 1

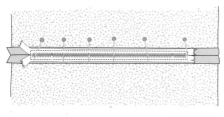

FIGURE 2

1. *measure + cut*

Cut 2 fabric pieces the exact dimensions of your pillow form. (You do not need a seam allowance; this pillow cover is slightly smaller than your form, which will create a plump finished pillow.)

2. *install the zipper*

POSITION AND PIN THE ZIPPER: On a flat surface, place the 2 pieces of fabric right sides together with raw edges aligned. Center the zipper on one side edge. Mark the zipper placement by inserting a pin in the fabric at each end of the zipper, just inside the caps. Put the zipper aside for now.

Sew the 2 layers of fabric together from the first corner to the first pin with a ½" (13mm) seam allowance. Backstitch (page 17), and change to a basting stitch (page 17). Baste until you reach the next pin, then backstitch, change to a normal stitch length, and sew to the corner. (FIGURE 1)

SEW THE ZIPPER: Press the seam allowance open. With the wrong side of the fabric facing up, align the zipper over the basted portion of the seam. Pin it in place. (FIGURE 2)

Attach a zipper foot to your machine. Beginning at one end of the zipper, sew up one side of the zipper, pivot and sew across the zipper, pivot and sew back down the other side, then pivot to sew across the zipper again. (FIGURE 2) For more information on installing a zipper, see the Don't Fear the Zipper sidebar.

Working on the right side of the pillow, use a seam ripper to gently remove the basting stitches and expose the zipper.

3. sew the pillow cover

Unzip the zipper, and fold the pillow in half, right sides together, at the zipper seam so that the remaining 3 raw edges are aligned; pin. Sew around all 3 sides with a ½" (13mm) seam allowance. (FIGURE 3)

Trim the corners (page 19) (FIGURE 3), and turn the pillow cover right side out through the zipper opening. Using a pointy tool, gently push out each corner. Press the corners and seams. Insert your pillow form and close the zipper.

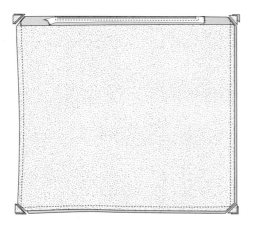

FIGURE 3

DON'T FEAR THE ZIPPER

Installing zippers strikes terror into the hearts of many sewers, even those who aren't beginners. But people, I'm here to tell you: The only thing you have to fear is fear itself.

Zippers really are easy to do. They're quick, and they can be quite painless—especially using my favorite method, which works whenever you are installing a standard zipper on a seam, like in this pillow cover. (Make sure you're using a standard zipper, not an "invisible" zipper, which requires a different installation method.) Here's how to do it.

1. Determine where on your seam you will place your zipper, and baste this portion of the seam closed. Sew the remainder of the seam with a regular stitch.
2. Pin the zipper right side down on the wrong side of the seam, centering the zipper teeth over the basted portion of the seam.
3. Load your machine with a zipper foot. Beginning at the top of the zipper, sew down one side of the zipper. When you reach the end of the zipper (just below the metal cap holding the teeth), pivot and sew across the zipper width, then pivot and sew up the other side of the zipper. If you're making a garment or other item where the top of the zipper will be open, stop here. If you're making a pillow or other item where the fabric above the zipper is closed: When you reach the top of the zipper (just above the zipper pull), pivot to sew across the width of the zipper again, ending when you reach the point where you began stitching, creating a complete rectangle of stitching. Backstitch to secure.
4. Working on the right side of the fabric, carefully remove the basting stitches with a seam ripper, and you're done! Enjoy your beautiful zipper, which is nearly invisible inside the seam.

15-minute *shams*

All it takes is one yard of fabric and some *cute trim* to whip up these *quick and easy* shams. French seams make them fully finished on the inside and outside, for *super-professional results*.

finished dimensions

LENGTH: 35" (89cm)
WIDTH: 17½" (44.5cm)

supplies

* Basic sewing supplies (page 11)
* **For one sham:**
    1 yard (91cm) medium-weight cotton
    1½ yard (1.4m) trim

1. *measure + cut*

For each pillow sham, cut a rectangle 36" x 41" (91cm x 104cm).

2. *sew the hem*

Turn under one of the 41" (104cm) edges ½" (2.5cm) and press. Turn that edge under again 5" (12.5cm) and press. Topstitch (page 17), sewing close to the inner folded edge.

3. *sew the side seams*

Fold the piece in half with wrong sides together, aligning the hemmed edge with itself and matching the 36" (91cm) raw edges. Sew the long side with a ¼" (6mm) French seam (page 13). Next, sew the remaining short edge with a ¼" (6mm) French seam.

Turn the case right side out and press.

4. *attach trim*

Using a hand-sewing needle, stitch the trim to the sham parallel to the hemmed edge of the sham, about 1" (2.5cm) from the edge.

make-it-your-way *ottoman cover*

Add some pop to your living room and turn an outdated ottoman into something *snazzy* with a simple DIY slipcover. This pattern shows you how to make a *custom cover* that's guaranteed to fit any ottoman like a glove. Not an ottoman person? You can also use this pattern to craft a cover for any boxy item, from a pet crate to an outdoor grill.

finished dimensions

Sized to fit any square or rectangular object

supplies

* Basic sewing supplies (page 11)
* Fabric (calculate yardage needed in Step 1)

fabric suggestions

Heavy decorator-weight cottons, canvas, duck cloth, microsuede, and upholstery fabrics are all great choices for this project. Oilcloth or outdoor fabrics are good choices for making an indoor-outdoor item like a grill cover. Lightweight fabrics are not recommended.

note

This project is sewn with ½" (13mm) seam allowances throughout. Normally you would add 1" (2.5cm) to the total width to allow for the seam allowance on both sides of each panel, but I've designed this cover with a slight amount of negative ease to keep the fit snug, so I'm only calling for an additional ¾" (2cm).

1. ## measure + cut

TOP AND SIDE PANELS: Measure the top and sides of your ottoman. *For the top panel*: Add ¾" (2cm) to the length and width for seam allowances. *For the side panels*: Add ¾" (2cm) to the width of each side piece and add 2" (5cm) to the height of each piece for seam allowances and hem.

Cut 4 side panels and one top panel to the dimensions you calculated above.

2. sew the side seams of the side panels

Starting from the top of each side panel and with right sides together, pin then sew each of the 4 side panel pieces together using ½" (13mm) seam allowances, forming a tube (FIGURE 1). (Be sure you are joining the length-measurement sides). Begin each seam ½" (13mm) from each top corner, and backstitch (page 17) to reinforce at the beginning and end of each seam. (FIGURE 1 INSET)

Turn the joined piece right side out and slip it over the ottoman to check for fit; it should fit snugly but not so tight that the fabric is pulling. If necessary, adjust by letting out or taking in the seams. Press the seams flat.

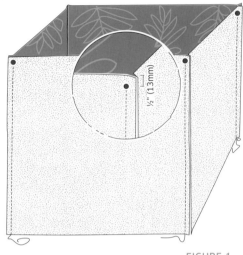

½" (13mm)

FIGURE 1

3. attach the top

Turn the joined side panels (made in Step 2) inside out. With right sides together, pin one side of the top panel to the edge of one side panel. Sew them together, beginning and ending the seam ½" (13mm) from each corner, backstitching to reinforce at the beginning and end of each seam. (FIGURE 2)

Repeat for the remaining 3 sides, sewing one side at a time, and taking care to smooth the top flat as you pin.

4. check the fit

Turn the cover right side out and slip it over the ottoman to check the fit, as you did in Step 2. Adjust any seams as necessary. While the cover s on the ottoman, turn under the bottom hem 1½" (3.8cm) and pin in place. If any shifting has occurred during sewing and the bottom edges are at all uneven, adjust for it now by pinning the hem so that the bottom edge is even and falls just above the floor.

5. clip the corners

Turn the cover inside out again and clip all the corner seam allowances (page 19). Using a pointy tool, gently push out each corner. Press all seams flat.

6. hem

Press the hem (which you turned under in Step 4), turning under the raw edge ½" (13mm) as you press. Topstitch (page 17) along the upper folded edge. Press the topstitching.

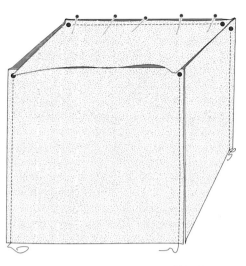

FIGURE 2

91

make-it-your-way ottoman cover

THIN ACCENT STRIPS: Cut 6 strips of fabric, each 36" (91cm) long and 2" (5cm) wide.

TOP AND BOTTOM STRIPS: Subtract the width of your center panel from measurement **B** and add 3½" (9cm). Divide this number in half for measurement **C**.

Cut 2 pieces of fabric that are as long as measurement **A** and as wide as measurement **C**.

BACK: Cut 2 strips of fabric that are as long as measurement **B** plus 3½" (9cm), and as wide as half measurement **A**.

2. assemble the thin accent strips

Pin then sew 3 of the thin accent strips together along the short edges using ¼" (6mm) French seams (page 18). Repeat to join the remaining 3 strips. Trim both strips so that they are as long as measurement A. (FIGURE 1)

3. assemble the front and back

Pin then sew together all of the strips for the front using ¼" (6mm) French seams. (Note that the seams will run horizontally on the front of the duvet.)

Pin then sew together the 2 strips for the back using ¼" (6mm) French seams. (Note that the seam will run vertically on the back of the duvet.)

4. hem the front and back

Hem the bottom edge of the front and the back as follows: Turn under the raw edge 1½" (3.8cm) and press. Turn under another 1½" (3.8cm) and press. Topstitch (page 17) close to both folded edges. (FIGURE 2)

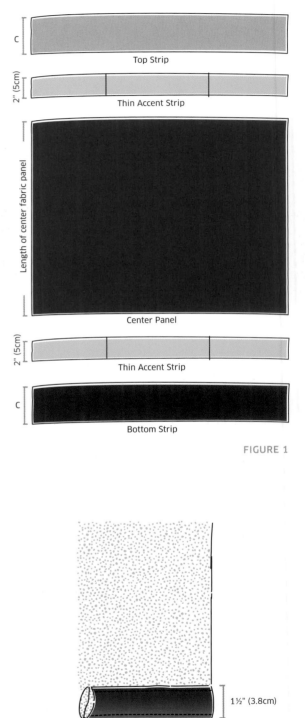

C — Top Strip

2" (5cm) — Thin Accent Strip

Length of center fabric panel — Center Panel

2" (5cm) — Thin Accent Strip

C — Bottom Strip

FIGURE 1

1½" (3.8cm)

FIGURE 2

5. *attach the front and back*

Pin the front to the back with wrong sides
together and all edges aligned. First sew the
side seams with ¼" (6mm) French seams,
then sew the top seam with a ¼" (6mm)
French seam. **(FIGURE 3)**

Turn the piece right side out. Press.

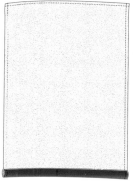

FIGURE 3

6. *make buttonholes and*
attach buttons

On the hem of the front of the duvet cover,
mark the desired placement for your
buttonholes, spacing them about 9" (23cm)
apart and centered within the hem allowance.
Make horizontal buttonholes, referring to
your sewing machine manual for instructions.
(FIGURE 4)

Close the duvet and mark the placement for
buttons on the hem of the back of the duvet
cover by marking through each buttonhole.
Sew a button to each mark.

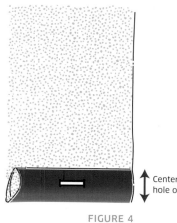

Center button-
hole on hem.

FIGURE 4

clutter-busting *bucket tote*

Clutter got you down? Corral household odds and ends with this *roomy container*. I use mine for yarn, but it's also great for toys, magazines, and general junk. Once you understand the basic construction of this piece you'll find it easy to *customize* this pattern to make a *tote* in any size, for anything you need!

finished dimensions

HEIGHT: 9½"(24cm) excluding handles
DIAMETER: 9½"(24cm)

supplies

* Basic sewing supplies (page 11)
* 1 yard (91cm) heavyweight fabric, such as canvas (for exterior)
* 1 yard (91cm) medium-weight fabric (for lining)
* 1 yard (91cm) heavy interfacing
* Corrugated plastic or plastic canvas, at least 6¾" x 7½" (17cm x 19cm)
* Hot glue gun

1. measure + cut

BODY AND LINING: Measure a rectangle that is 16" x 15" (40.5cm x 38cm). Cut 2 pieces from the exterior fabric, 2 from the lining fabric, and 4 from the interfacing.

Orient each piece so the 16" (40.5cm) edges are the top and bottom. Cut a 4" (10cm) square from the 2 bottom corners of each piece.

STRAPS: Measure a rectangle that is 11" x 2¼" (28cm x 5.5cm). Cut 2 from the exterior fabric and 2 from the lining fabric.

PLASTIC BOTTOM LINER (BASE): Measure and cut a 6¾" x 7½" (17cm x 19cm) rectangle from the corrugated plastic. **(FIGURE 1)**

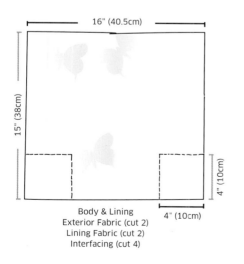

16" (40.5cm)

15" (38cm)

4" (10cm)

4" (10cm)

Body & Lining
Exterior Fabric (cut 2)
Lining Fabric (cut 2)
Interfacing (cut 4)

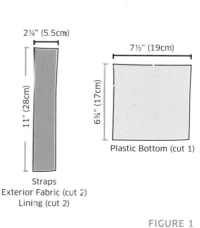

2¼" (5.5cm)

11" (28cm)

Straps
Exterior Fabric (cut 2)
Lining (cut 2)

7½" (19cm)

6¾" (17cm)

Plastic Bottom (cut 1)

FIGURE 1

2. *make the straps*

On each strap piece (2 exterior fabric, 2 lining), turn under one long (11" [28cm]) edge ½" (13mm), and press. Pin one exterior-fabric strap piece to one lining-fabric strap piece with right sides together and raw and folded edges aligned. Sew the pieces together along the unfolded 11" (28cm) edge, using a ½" (13mm) seam allowance. (FIGURE 2)

Fold the piece in half along the seam with *wrong* sides together and press on the fold (remember that the other 11" [28cm] edges were already folded and pressed). Topstitch (page 17) along each 11" (28cm) side, stitching close to the edges. (FIGURE 3)

3. *assemble the body and lining*

Fuse a piece of interfacing (page 19) to both of the exterior body fabric pieces and both lining pieces.

Pin the 2 exterior body pieces with right sides together and all edges even. Sew the 2 side seams and the bottom seam using a ½" (13mm) seam allowance. (FIGURE 4) Press the seam allowances open.

TO MAKE THE CORNERS on the exterior of the tote, fold the piece, right sides together, so that the side and bottom *seams* meet; pin. Sew with a ½" (13mm) seam allowance. (FIGURE 5) Trim the corners (page 19), turn right side out, and press the seams.

Repeat Step 3 to assemble the lining in the same way.

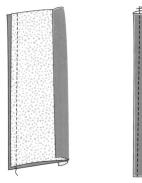

FIGURE 2   FIGURE 3

FIGURE 4

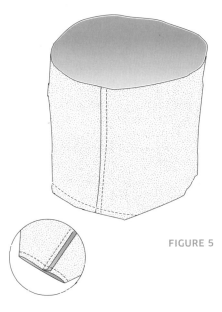

FIGURE 5

cozy, crafty home

4. attach the bottom (base)

Place the 6¾" x 7½" (17cm x 19cm) plastic bottom liner inside the bottom of the tote body exterior, slipping it under the seam allowances. Using a hot glue gun, glue the seam allowances to the plastic (to keep the plastic from shifting later).

5. attach the straps

Position and pin the right sides of the straps to the right side of the tote body exterior, (the lining side of the straps will face out). Position each end of the straps 2" (5cm) from the side seams, and align the raw edges of the straps with the raw edges of the tote body. Sew the straps in place with a ¼" (6mm) seam allowance. (FIGURE 6)

6. finish the tote

Turn under the raw edge of the exterior ½" (13mm) and press. Turn under the raw edge of the lining ½" (13mm) and press. With the body exterior *right* side out and the lining *wrong* side out, place the lining inside the exterior, aligning the folded top edges (the straps will be sticking up and sandwiched between the exterior and lining fabrics). Pin the pieces together. Load your machine with a heavy-duty needle and topstitch the exterior and lining together, stitching close to the folded top edges all the way around. (FIGURE 7)

FIGURE 6

FIGURE 7

pixelated *throw*

Staggered strips and wonky squares create a *bold, graphic look* in this quilt that reminds me of an eighties-era video game. I think that makes it a perfect choice for the geeks and guys in your life—who says *quilts* have to be girly? (Although, if you stitched this in a softer color palette, it would take on a much fairer look.) A patchwork back means it's *reversible too*, so no matter which way you throw it, this quilt will look great!

finished dimensions
WIDTH: Approximately 42" (106.5cm)
LENGTH: Approximately 64" (163cm)

supplies
* Basic sewing supplies (page 11)
* 2½ yards (2.3m) medium-weight cotton of each color (for background and binding): light gray, dark gray
* 1 yard (91cm) orange medium-weight cotton
* ½ yard (46cm) medium yellow medium-weight cotton
* ¼ yard (23cm) medium-weight cotton of each color: red, light yellow, dark yellow
* 2 yards (1.8m) complementary gray print fabric for quilt back
* 70" x 50" (178cm x 127cm) piece medium-loft cotton batting

note

The tiny squares on this quilt have an off-kilter wonky construction. For technical ease, I give measurements that make perfect squares rather than wonky ones. For the wonky look, cut the small squares *larger* than the sizes given (about 1" [2.5cm] on all sides), then sew your seams off-kilter. Some pieces may end up larger than the dimensions given here; when assembling the strips, just trim any large pieces to the correct size for piecing to their neighbors. Because this quilt has an abstract quality, it won't matter if your elements are slightly different from the pattern. Have fun with it!

1. *measure + cut*

Referring to **FIGURE 1** (opposite) and **FIGURE 2** (page 104), cut each numbered piece to the measurements given below (horizontal x vertical) from the indicated fabric color.

quilt front

1. dark gray, 42" x 3" (106.5cm x 7.5cm)

2. dark gray, 6¾" x 3" (17cm x 7.5cm)

3. red, 3" x 3" (7.5cm x 7.5cm)

4. dark gray, 33½" x 3" (85cm x 7.5cm)

5. dark gray, 27" x 3½" (68.5cm x 9cm)

6. medium yellow, 2½" x 2" (6.5cm x 5cm)

7. dark gray, 2½" x 2" (6.5cm x 5cm)

8. dark gray, 13½" x 3½" (34.5cm x 9cm)

9. dark gray, 11" x 3" (28cm x 7.5cm)

10. red, 3" x 3" (7.5cm x 7.5cm)

11. dark gray, 29" x 3" (74cm x 7.5cm)

12. dark gray, 42" x 2½" (106.5cm x 6.5cm)

13. dark gray, 4½" x 3½" (11.5cm x 9cm)

14. dark yellow, 2½" x 2½" (6.5cm x 6.5cm)

15. dark gray, 2½" x 2" (6.5cm x 5cm)

16. dark gray, 2½" x 3½" (6.5cm x 9cm)

17. dark gray, 1" x 2" (2.5cm x 5cm)

18. orange, 3" x 2" (7.5cm x 5cm)

19. dark gray, 3½" x 3½" (9cm x 9cm)

20. medium yellow, 2½" x 3½" (6.5cm x 9cm)

21. dark gray, 27½" x 3½" (70cm x 9cm)

22. dark gray, 42" x 3" (106.5cm x 7.5cm)

23. dark gray, 7" x 2½" (18cm x 6.5cm)

24. light yellow, 3½" x 2½" (9cm x 6.5cm)

25. dark gray, 3" x 2½" (7.5cm x 6.5cm)

26. dark gray, 2" x 1" (5cm x 2.5cm)

27. medium yellow, 2½" x 2" (6.5cm x 5cm)

28. dark gray, 28½" x 2½" (72cm x 6.5cm)

29. dark gray, 42" x 2½" (106.5cm x 6.5cm)

30. dark gray, 19½" x 4½" (49.5cm x 11.5cm)

31. light yellow, 23" x 4½" (58.5cm x 11.5cm)

32. medium yellow, 25" x 5" (63.5cm x 12.5cm)

33. light gray, 17½" x 5" (44.5cm x 12.5cm)

34. dark gray, 6½" x 3½" (16.5cm x 9cm)

35. light yellow, 11" x 3½" (28cm x 9cm)

36. dark yellow, 25½" x 3½" x (65cm x 9cm)

37. medium yellow, 10" x 4" (25.5cm x 10cm)

38. light yellow, 24½" x 4" (62cm x 10cm)

39. light gray, 8½" x 4" (21.5cm x 10cm)

40. light gray, 17½" x 2½" (44.5cm x 6.5cm)

41. orange, 25" x 2½" (63.5cm x 6.5cm)

42. light gray, 42" x 2½" (106.5cm x 6.5cm)

43. light gray, 15" x 4" (38cm x 10cm)

44. light gray, 2" x 2" (5cm x 5cm)

45. orange, 2" x 2½" (5cm x 6.5cm)

46. light gray, 10" x 4" (25.5cm x 10cm)

47. light yellow, 16½" x 4" (42cm x 10cm)

48. light gray, 42" x 3" (106.5cm x 7.5cm)

49. light gray, 11" x 4" (28cm x 10cm)

50. light gray, 2" x 2" (5cm x 5cm)

51. red, 2 x 2½" (5cm x 6.5cm)

52. light gray, 6" x 4" (15cm x 10cm)

53. light gray, 3" x 1½" (7.5cm x 3.8cm)

54. orange, 3" x 2½" (7.5cm x 6.5cm)

55. light gray, 3" x 1" (7.5cm x 2.5cm)

56. light gray, 3" x 4" (7.5cm x 10cm)

57. orange, 20½" x 4" (52cm x 10cm)

58. light gray, 42" x 3" (106.5cm x 7.5cm)

59. light gray, 24½" x 2½" (62cm x 6.5cm)

60. dark yellow, 2½" x 2½" (6.5cm x 6.5cm)

61. light gray, 4" x 2½" (10cm x 6.5cm)

62. light gray, 2½" x 1" (6.5cm x 2.5cm)

63. orange, 2½" x 2" (6.5cm x 5cm)

64. light gray, 10½" x 2½" (26.5cm x 6.5cm)

65. light gray, 42" x 2" (106.5cm x 5cm)

66. light gray, 14½" x 2½" (37cm x 6.5cm)

67. medium yellow, 3" x 2½" (7.5cm x 6.5cm)

68. light gray, 15" x 2½" (38cm x 6.5cm)

69. medium yellow, 2½" x 2½" (6.5cm x 6.5cm)

70. light gray, 9" x 2½" (23cm x 6.5cm)

71. light gray, 34" x 3" (86cm x 7.5cm)

72. red, 3" x 3" (7.5cm x 7.5cm)

73. light gray, 6" x 3" (15cm x 7.5cm)

74. light gray, 42" x 3" (106.5cm x 7.5cm)

cozy, crafty home

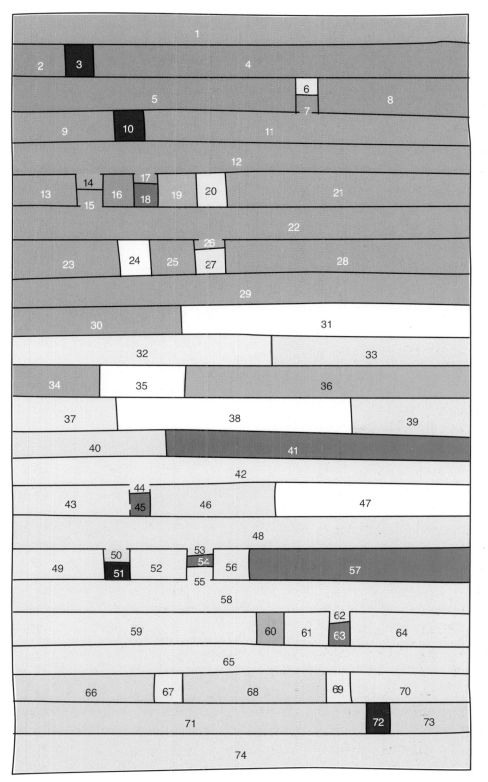

FIGURE 1 (QUILT FRONT)

quilt back

75. gray print, 20" x 70" (51cm x 178cm)

76. medium yellow, 10½" x 18" (26.5cm x 45.5cm)

77. orange, 10½" x 27½" (26.5cm x 70cm)

78. red, 10½" x 6" (26.5cm x 15cm)

79. orange, 10½" x 20" (26.5cm x 51cm)

80. gray print, 20" x 70" (51cm x 178cm)

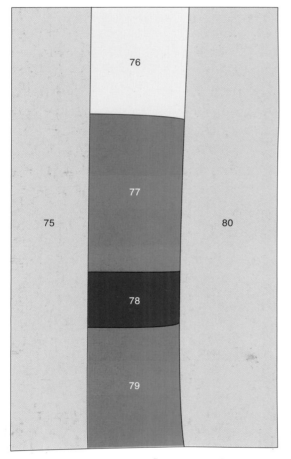

FIGURE 2 (QUILT BACK)

2. assemble strips for the quilt front

Assemble each horizontal strip for the quilt front as shown in the Quilt Front diagram. (FIGURE 1) If the strip contains a pieced square, sew that first and then join it to its neighboring strips. Sew all the pieces with right sides together, using a ¼" (6mm) seam allowance. (If you are sewing wonky lines as described in the note on page 101, you will use larger seam allowances.) Press all the seam allowances to one side, facing the same direction.

Once all the horizontal strips are complete, join the strips to each other vertically. With right sides together, pin then sew with ¼" (6mm) seam allowances. Press all the seams to one side, facing in the same direction.

3. square the quilt top

If you decided to go the wonky route, your quilt's sides may not be perfectly even. To square up your quilt top, use a straightedge and a rotary cutter or scissors to trim the sides of the quilt to make all sides even and all 4 corners right angles.

4. assemble strips for the quilt back

Refer to FIGURE 2. Assemble the vertical back center strip, pinning then sewing the pieces with right sides together and using ¼" (6mm) seam allowances. Press all the seam allowances to one side, facing in the same direction. Pin then sew one of the gray side strips to each long side of the center strip, using ¼" (6mm) seam allowances. Press the seam allowances to one side, facing in the same direction.

5. layer and baste the quilt

Place the assembled quilt back on a floor or work surface with the wrong side facing up. Layer the batting on top of it, being sure to smooth out any wrinkles. Center the quilt front over the batting, with the right side of quilt front facing up. The front will be smaller than the batting and quilt back).

Using a hand-sewing needle and thread, baste (page 15) all 3 layers of the quilt together using long running stitches (approximately 3" [7.5cm] long), placed approximately 6" (15cm) apart. Alternatively, you can pin the layers together with safety pins.

6. quilt the quilt

With a neutral color thread (I used white), sew quilting lines horizontally across the quilt (page 21), slanting or crisscrossing the lines randomly.

7. finish

Trim the quilt back and batting so the edges are even with the quilt front.

tip

Flip to page 21 for lots more info on layering, basting, binding, and quilting your quilt.

8. bind the quilt

Refer to the instructions on page 22 to make and attach the quilt binding to finish the raw edges.

Optional: If you like, make a 2-toned binding so that the light gray portion of the quilt gets a light gray binding, and the dark gray gets a dark gray binding. To do this, attach one color binding first, starting and stopping about 12" (30.5cm) inside the point where the colors change. Join the second color binding to the first aligning the join with the point on the quilt top where the colors change, then continue attaching the binding.

wonky diamonds on point

When it comes to quilts, I love bright colors set on neutral backgrounds, with lots of *crazy lines*. In this design, I wanted to set diamonds on the diagonal, which calls for precision, yet I got my crazy fix by adding a wonky center to each *diamond piece*. The result is a *quilt* that combines a little bit of everything, and while it only requires straight-line sewing, the construction offers a bit of a challenge—for those who like that sort of thing!

finished dimensions

WIDTH: 81" (205.5cm)
LENGTH 90" (229cm) (fits a double/queen bed)

supplies

* Basic sewing supplies (page 11)
* ¼ yard (23cm) each:

    10 patterned fabrics (for diamond centers)

    20 coordinating solid fabrics (for diamonds)

* 6 yards (5.5m) white fabric
* 6 yards (5.5m) coordinating solid or patterned fabric (for quilt back)
* 5 large sheets of card stock for templates, each measuring at least 15" x 12" (38cm x 30.5cm)
* 87" x 96" (221cm x 244cm) piece medium-loft cotton batting

fabric suggestions

Quilting cottons are perfect for this project. They are just the right weight, and come in a wide array of colors.

1. measure + cut

NOTE: To avoid confusion, label the fabric pieces as you cut them.

TEMPLATES: Using the templates on pages 113–117, enlarge them 200% and transfer the enlarged templates onto card stock, and cut them out. *Transfer all template markings to your card stock templates.*

FABRIC: *Be sure to cut your fabric in the order listed below.* (This will ensure you'll have enough fabric to cut the longest pieces.)

TOP/BOTTOM BORDERS: From the white fabric, cut two 8" x 81" (20.5cm x 205.5cm) rectangles.

SIDE BORDERS: From the white fabric, cut two 11" x 74" (28cm x 188cm) rectangles.

LONG SASHING (NO TEMPLATE): From the white fabric, cut the following strips:

Long Sashing **X:** Two 3½" x 40" (9cm x 101.5cm) strips
Long Sashing **Y:** Two 3½" x 65" (9cm x 165cm) strips
Long Sashing **Z:** Two 3½" x 85" (9cm x 216cm) strips

SHORT SASHING: From the white fabric, cut 30 pieces of short sashing, using the Short Sashing template.

BORDER TRIANGLES A: Cut 2 from the right side and 2 from the wrong side of the white fabric, using the Border Triangle **A** template.

BORDER TRIANGLES B: Cut 6 from the white fabric, using the Border Triangle **B** template.

BORDER TRIANGLES C: Cut 4 from the white fabric using the Border Triangle **C** template.

WONKY DIAMOND CENTERS (NO TEMPLATE): From the assorted patterned fabrics, cut 25 center squares, each measuring 5" x 5" (12.5cm x 12.5cm). These are the center of the diamonds, which will be attached to the solid diamond borders.

WONKY DIAMOND BORDERS D AND E (NO TEMPLATE): From the assorted solids, cut fifty 5" x 5" (12.5cm x 12.5cm) pieces (**D**) and fifty 5" x 10" (12.5cm x 25.5cm) pieces (**E**). These are the solid portion of the diamonds, which will be attached to the diamond centers.

QUILT BACK: Cut two 44" x 96" pieces (112cm x 244cm) from the quilt back fabric.

2. make 25 wonky diamond blocks

Since the diamonds are sewn with wonky seams, you don't need to worry about sewing each one perfectly.

With right sides together, pin one raw edge of a Wonky Diamond Border **D** to one raw edge of a Wonky Diamond Center. To get the wonky effect, sew the pieces unevenly using one of these methods: 1) Place the raw edges slightly askew and then sew a straight, even seam (seam allowances will vary according to your wonkiness), or 2) Match the raw edges evenly but vary your seam allowance from wider to narrower as you sew. (FIGURE 1)

Repeat to attach another Wonky Diamond Border **D** to the opposite side of the Wonky Diamond Center. (FIGURE 2) Trim the seam allowances to ¼" (6mm), and press them to one side. (If one fabric is lighter in color, press the seam allowance toward the darker fabric to prevent the darker allowance showing through the lighter fabric.)

Sew a Wonky Diamond Border **E** to each of
the long raw edges of the diamond piece you
constructed above, again sewing a wonky
seam. Trim the seam allowances to ¼' (6mm),
and press them in one direction. (FIGURE 3)

Next, trim the resulting piece to the correct
size using the Diamond template. Place the
Diamond template over the joined diamond
piece, situating the (fabric) diamond center
approximately in the center of the template.
Using a rotary cutter and straightedge, trim the
diamond so that all edges are even with the
template. (FIGURE 4) The resulting piece is one
finished diamond. (FIGURE 5)

Transfer all corner dots from the Diamond
Template to the finished diamond block.
Repeat to create all 25 diamond blocks.

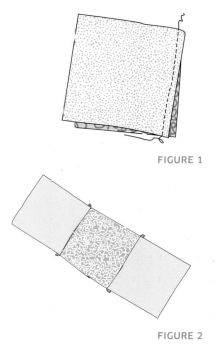

FIGURE 1

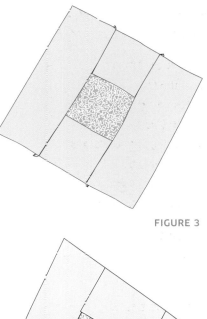

FIGURE 2

FIGURE 3

wonky diamonds on point

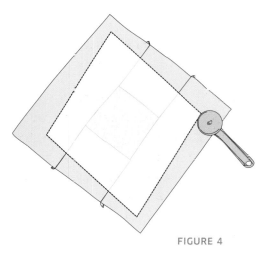

FIGURE 4

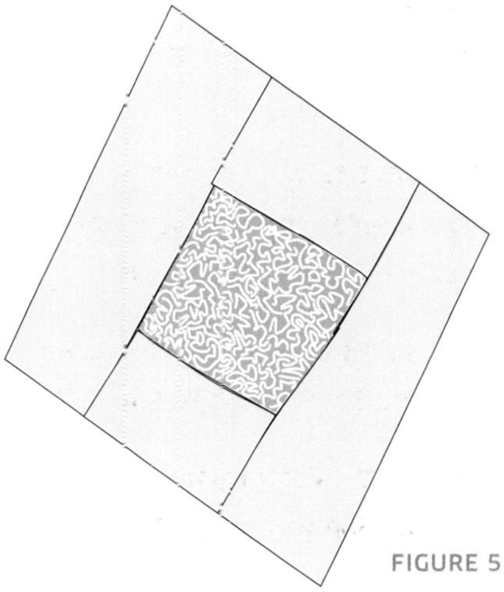

FIGURE 5

3. arrange diamond blocks

Arrange the 25 diamond blocks on a floor, bed, or work surface, placing colors as you desire. Referring to FIGURE 6, number each diamond according to its placement so you don't lose track of the layout once you start sewing. (I find it easiest to write the number on a small scrap of paper and pin it to the diamond.)

4. assemble the 7 strips

NOTE: For the remainder of this quilt's construction, the seams should be sewn straight and even, not wonky. Always sew fabrics right sides together with a ¼" (6mm) seam allowance.

Refer to FIGURE 6. Beginning where indicated for Strip 1, assemble the Diamonds, Short Sashing, and Border Triangles into 7 strips. Pin pieces together before sewing them, aligning the corner dots. For the angles to work out correctly, sew each strip in the order specified below.

SEW STRIP 1 IN THIS ORDER: Border Triangle C, Short Sashing, Diamond 1, Short Sashing, Border Triangle B.

SEW STRIP 2 IN THIS ORDER: Border Triangle C, Short Sashing, Diamond 2, Short Sashing, Diamond 3, Short Sashing, Diamond 4, Short Sashing, Border Triangle B.

Sew Strips 3–7 in the same manner, following the order specified above. Once the 7 strips are assembled, press all seam allowances in the same direction.

5. join the strips with long sashing

Once all 7 strips are assembled, join them with the Long Sashing pieces. Begin at the top left of the quilt. Situate Strip 1 facing right side up, and align and pin Long Sashing X along the longer edge of Strip 1. (The sashing will be longer than the strip; center it so that the overhang is equal on each end). Stitch the seam and press the seam allowance to one side.

Next, place the joined strip and sashing right side up, and mark as follows: Refer to FIGURE 7 (page 112). With chalk or a disappearing pen, draw a line from each short sashing seam across the long sashing. Mark a line ¼" (6mm) in from the long raw edge of the long sashing. Mark a dot at the spot where these lines intersect.

Along the neighboring edge of the next strip to be joined, mark a dot at each seam ¼" (6mm) in from the raw edge.

Place these two sections right sides together, aligning all dots. Pin, then sew; press the seam allowance to one side.

Continue to join all strips in this manner, using the length of long sashing indicated in FIGURE 6. The long sashing will overhang on the sides of the quilt. When all the strips are assembled, trim the sashing overhang so that it is flush with the rest of the quilt top.

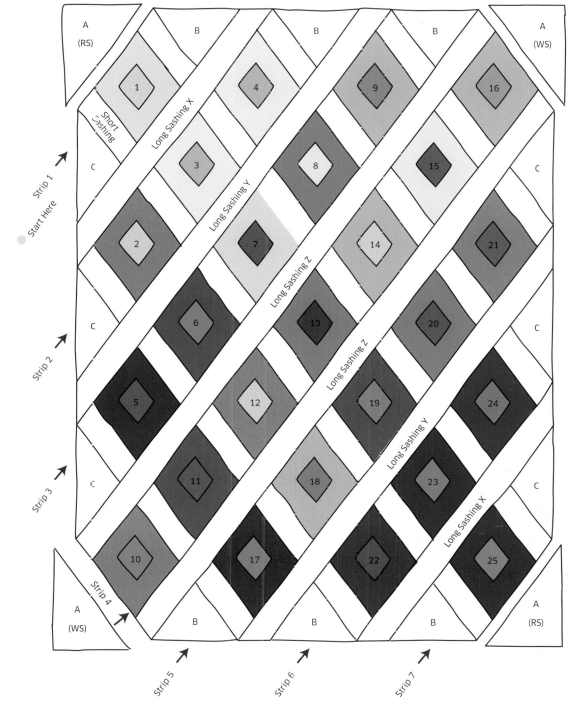

FIGURE 6: CONSTRUCTION DIAGRAM

6. add the corner triangles

Pin then sew the Border Triangle A pieces to the corners of the quilt, being sure to place the right side/wrong side pieces correctly according to FIGURE 6.

7. add the border

Pin then sew an 11" x 74" (28cm x 188cm) side border piece to each of the 2 side edges of the quilt top, using ¼" (6mm) seam allowances. Press the seam allowances to one side.

Pin then sew an 8" x 81" (20.5cm x 205.5cm) border piece to the top and bottom edges of the quilt, and press the seam allowances to one side.

8. assemble the quilt back

Arrange the two 44" x 96" (112cm x 244cm) pieces with right sides together and the long sides aligned; pin. Sew, and press the seam allowance to one side.

9. layer and quilt

Place the quilt back on a floor or work surface with the wrong side facing up. Place the batting over this, smoothing to remove any wrinkles. Center the quilt top over this, with the right side facing up. (The quilt top will be smaller than the quilt back and batting.)

tip

Visit my website, www.brettbara.com, for more helpful tips and tricks.

tip

It can be difficult to quilt large pieces like this on a home sewing machine. Many people choose to send their quilt out to be quilted professionally on a special quilting machine. Most local quilt shops offer this service or can recommend someone who does, so ask at your local shop!

Using a hand-sewing needle and thread, baste all 3 layers of the quilt together using long running stitches (approximately 3" [7.5cm] long), placed approximately 6" (15cm) apart. Alternatively, you can pin the layers together with safety pins.

Quilt through all layers (page 21) using the photograph on page 107 as a guide, or in any pattern you desire. (Simple diagonal crisscrossing lines would look great, too!)

10. bind the quilt

Please see page 22 for detailed instructions on making and attaching quilt binding. Make a 440" (11.2m) length of binding, and attach it as instructed.

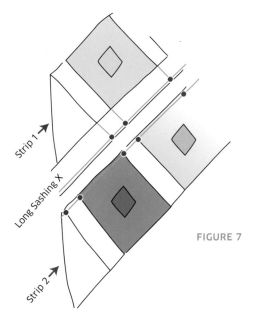

Strip 1

Long Sashing X

Strip 2

FIGURE 7

cozy, crafty home

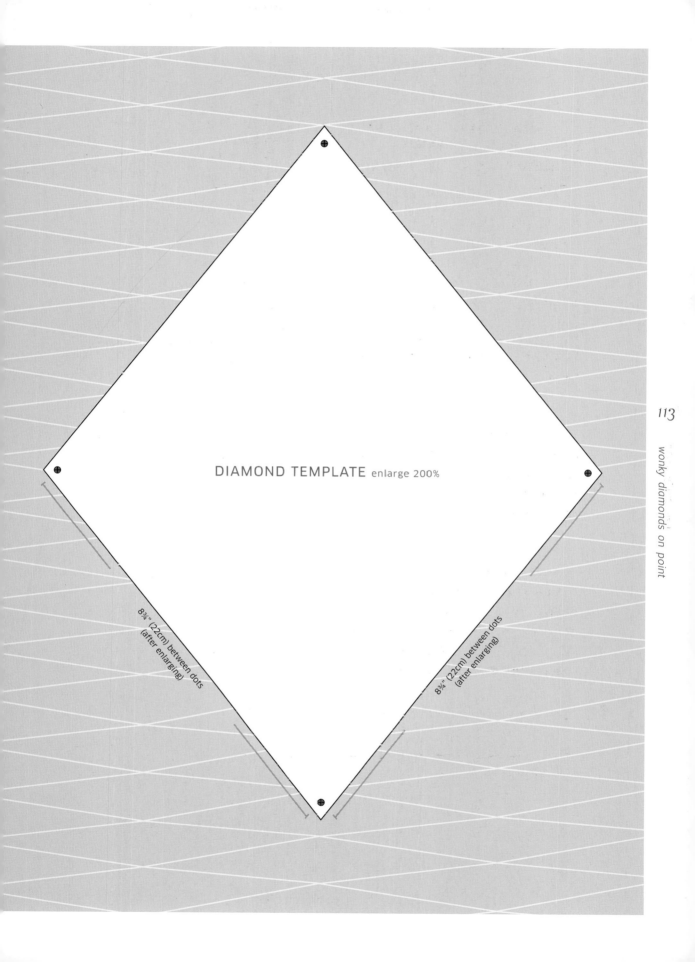

DIAMOND TEMPLATE enlarge 200%

8¾" (22cm) between dots
(after enlarging)

8¾" (22cm) between dots
(after enlarging)

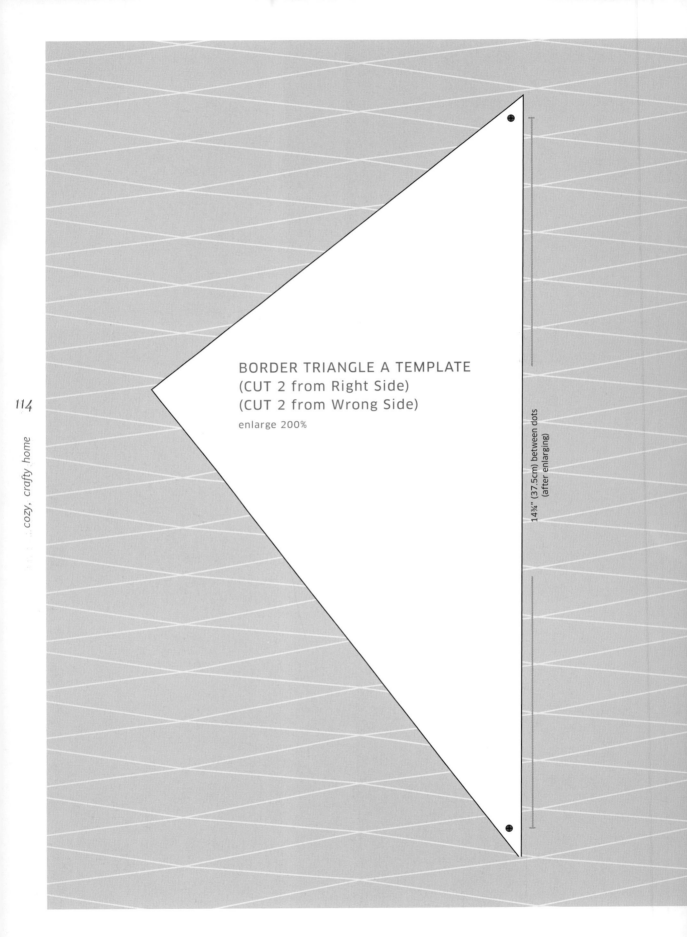

BORDER TRIANGLE A TEMPLATE
(CUT 2 from Right Side)
(CUT 2 from Wrong Side)
enlarge 200%

14¾" (37.5cm) between dots
(after enlarging)

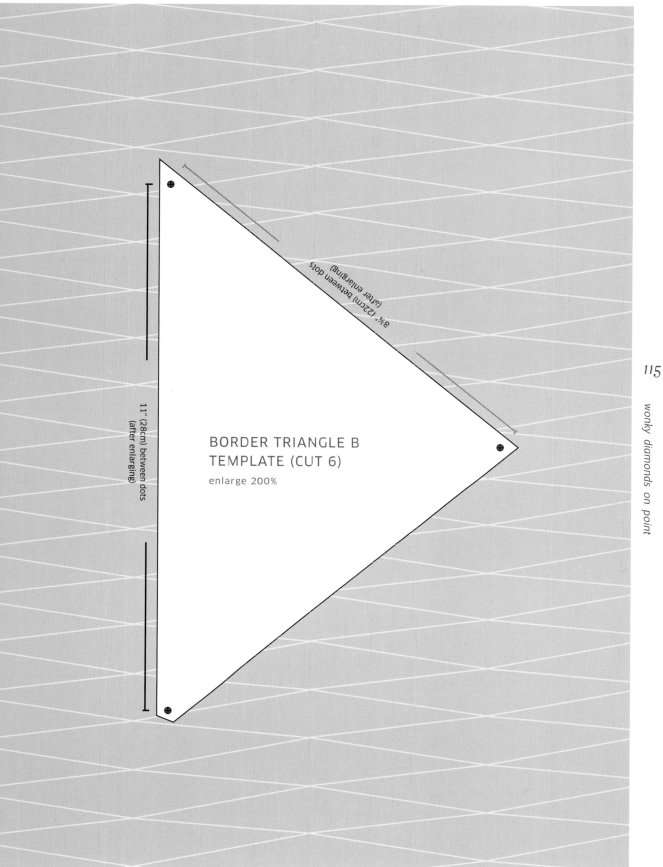

BORDER TRIANGLE B
TEMPLATE (CUT 6)

enlarge 200%

11" (28cm) between dots
(after enlarging)

8¾" (22cm) between dots
(after enlarging)

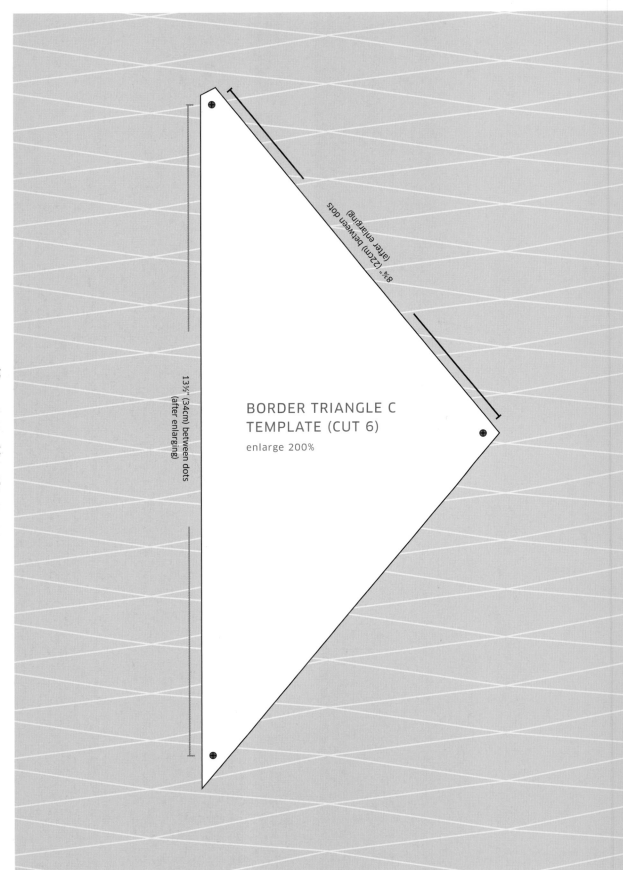

BORDER TRIANGLE C
TEMPLATE (CUT 6)
enlarge 200%

8¾" (22cm) between dots
(after enlarging)

13½" (34cm) between dots
(after enlarging)

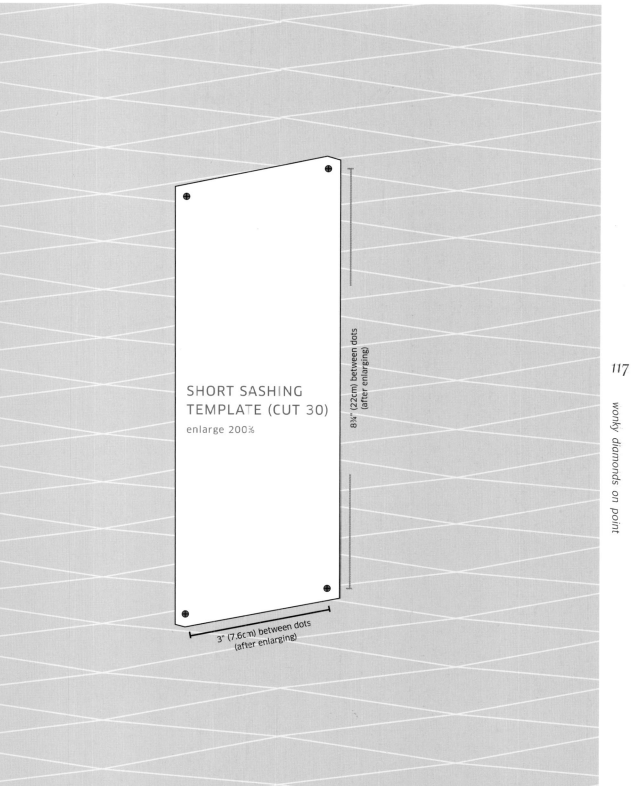

SHORT SASHING
TEMPLATE (CUT 30)
enlarge 200%

8¾" (22cm) between dots
(after enlarging)

3" (7.6cm) between dots
(after enlarging)

quick, cute gifts

Holidays, birthdays, and other gifting events mean only one thing to me: *time to get crafty*! I love to give handmade presents whenever possible.

You don't need advanced skills or tons of time to sew a *gift* that's truly *special*. Just about everything in this chapter can be made with basic skills and a free afternoon—all you need to create amazing gifts their recipients are *sure to love*.

In this section you'll find *sweet*, quick *projects* for everyone in your life—men, ladies, and little ones, too. Some of the projects are crazy easy, like the Folded Flower Bowls and 60-Second Hello. Once you've mastered the basics, move on to the On-the-Go Jewelry Keeper or Staggering Strips Baby Quilt for presents that are *just perfect*.

And if you like a bit of a *challenge*, Mister Bunny and Miss Kitty are a charming pair of softies for kids or kids at heart, while the Denim Dop Bag is *just*

right for tough guys who can be tricky to craft for. The 9-to-5 Folder is great for work friends, and the Magic Sewing Kit just might get my vote for all-time favorite crafty gift.

Many of these projects can be made from fabric leftovers in your stash, or from very small amounts of purchased fabric. That means you don't have to spend much money to *give a gift* that means a ton.

So for perfect presents that are fun to make and easy on your wallet too, look no further than the very next page. **Let's go!**

folded *flower bowls*

Can you believe these **round bowls** are made with straight seams? A simple square turns into a *flower-like vessel* with a little nip-tuck at the corners. Best of all, each one takes mere minutes to make. **Try it**—I bet you can't stitch just one!

finished dimensions

small bowl
WIDTH: 3¾" (9.5cm)
HEIGHT: 1¾" (4.5cm)

medium bowl:
WIDTH: 5" (13.5cm)
HEIGHT: 2" (5cm)

large bowl:
WIDTH: 6" (16cm)
HEIGHT: 2¼" (5.5cm)

supplies

* Basic sewing supplies (page 11)
* ¼ yard (23cm) each of 4 medium-weight fabrics, such as quilting cottons, in coordinating colors (for small and medium bowls)
* ⅓ yard (30cm) each of 2 medium-weight fabrics, such as quilting cottons, in coordinating colors (for large bowl)
* ½ yard (46cm) heavyweight fusible interfacing

1. **measure + cut**

SMALL BOWL: Cut a 6½" (16.5cm) square from each of 2 coordinating fabrics, and 2 squares of the same size from interfacing.

MEDIUM BOWL: Cut an 8½" (21.5cm) square from each of 2 remaining coordinating fabrics, and 2 squares of the same size from interfacing.

LARGE BOWL: Cut a 9½" (24cm) square from each of the 2 remaining coordinating fabrics, and 2 squares of the same size from interfacing.
(FIGURE 1)

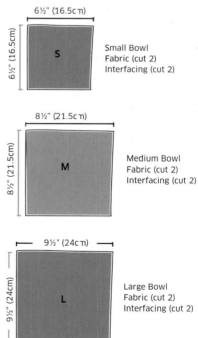

6½" (16.5cm)
6½" (16.5cm)
S
Small Bowl
Fabric (cut 2)
Interfacing (cut 2)

8½" (21.5cm)
8½" (21.5cm)
M
Medium Bowl
Fabric (cut 2)
Interfacing (cut 2)

9½" (24cm)
9½" (24cm)
L
Large Bowl
Fabric (cut 2)
Interfacing (cut 2)

FIGURE 1

2. *attach interfacing*

Fuse one corresponding piece of interfacing
(page 19) to the wrong side of each piece
of fabric.

3. *sew the squares*

Pin both small bowl (6½" [16.5cm]) squares
of fabric right sides together, aligning all raw
edges. Sew around all 4 sides with a ¼" (6mm)
seam allowance, leaving a 4" (10cm) opening
on one side. **(FIGURE 2)**

Trim the seam allowance from the corners
(page 19) and turn the piece right side out
through the opening in the stitching. Use a
pointy tool to carefully poke the corners out.
Turn under the raw edge of the fabric at the
opening ¼" (6mm) and press to the inside.
Topstitch (page 17) around all 4 sides, ½" from
the edge. **(FIGURE 3)**

Repeat Step 3 using the remaining pieces of
fabric to sew the medium and large squares.

4. *make the corners*

SMALL BOWL: Fold the square in half diagonally.
Mark a point along the side edge 1" (2.5cm)
in from the point of one folded corner, and
sew a seam from the folded edge to this spot,
perpendicular to the sides of the square.
(FIGURE 4) Repeat for all remaining corners of
the small bowl. As you sew each corner, the
bowl will begin to take shape.

MEDIUM BOWL: Fold and sew the corners as you
did for the small bowl, placing the seam 1½"
(3.8cm) from the point of the corner. **(FIGURE 4)**

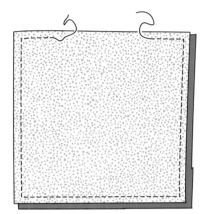

FIGURE 2

FIGURE 3

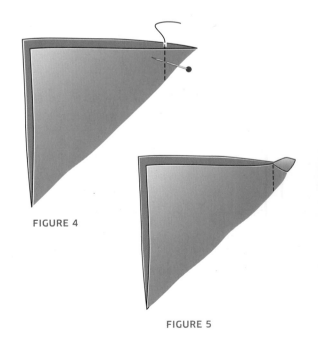

FIGURE 4

FIGURE 5

LARGE BOWL: Fold and sew the corners as you did for the small bowl, placing the seam 1¾" (4.5cm) from the point of the corner. **(FIGURE 4)**

FOR ALL SIZES: Open the tuck between the corner seam and the point of each corner. **(FIGURE 5)** Flatten the tuck out against the corner seam so that the corner point is centered on the seam. Topstitch the fabric in place across the fold, sewing parallel to the top edge of the bowl, about ¼" (6mm) from the edge, and backstitch to reinforce the seam. Repeat for every corner on each bowl. **(FIGURE 6)**

FIGURE 6

staggering strips *baby quilt*

Thanks to their small scale, *baby quilts* are the perfect platform for experimenting with color and layout. In this quilt, uneven strips of fabric are stitched together at staggered intervals, making a very *simple construction* look high-design. No exact measuring or precise cutting is required for this project, so you get all the crafty fun without all the fuss. You can finish this quilt in about a weekend, so if you need a quick gift that looks like it stepped out of a *modern boutique*—baby, this one's for you.

finished dimensions
WIDTH: Approximately 36" (91cm)
LENGTH: Approximately 30" (76cm)
(Because this quilt is imprecise, exact finished measurements will vary.)

supplies
* Basic sewing supplies (page 11)
* ¼ yard (23cm) each of 6 different fabrics in color group **A** (here, orange was used)
* ¼ yard (23cm) each of 6 different fabrics in a contrasting color group **B** (here, green was used)
* ½ yard (46cm) each of 3 fabrics in neutral tones for color group **C**
* 1 yard (91cm) coordinating fabric for quilt back
* ½ yard (46cm) coordinating fabric for binding
* 1 yard (91cm) cotton quilt batting

fabric suggestions
Quilting cottons are ideal for this project. Cotton-linen blends work nicely for the quilt back, if you like.

note

This project involves a little bit of randomness—exact measurements aren't necessary, so I encourage you to be free when cutting and stitching for a result that's all you.

1. *measure + cut*

Cut the **A**, **B**, and **C** fabrics into strips 2½"
(6.5cm) wide, and ranging in length from 13"
to 15" (33cm–38cm). You will need 11 strips
in color group **A**, 10 strips in color group **B**,
and 42 strips in color group **C** to make a quilt
just like this one—but of course you can vary
the number of each color strips you use for a
personalized design. **(FIGURE 1)**

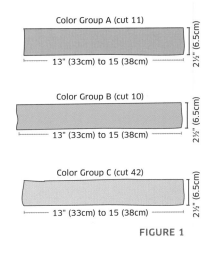

Color Group A (cut 11)
13" (33cm) to 15" (38cm) — 2½" (6.5cm)

Color Group B (cut 10)
13" (33cm) to 15" (38cm) — 2½" (6.5cm)

Color Group C (cut 42)
13" (33cm) to 15" (38cm) — 2½" (6.5cm)

FIGURE 1

2. *sew the strips of the quilt front*

Sew a **C** (neutral fabric) strip onto each short
end of every **A** and **B** strip. Press all seam
allowances toward the **A** and **B** sections so the
colored seam allowances don't show through
the lighter fabrics. **(FIGURE 2)**

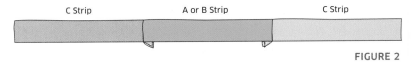

C Strip   A or B Strip   C Strip

FIGURE 2

3. *arrange the strips*

Lay out all the strips on your work surface
or floor. Arrange them, right side up, in the
color order you prefer. (I clustered my strips
in sections with orange at the top and bottom
and green in the middle.)

Arrange the strips so that the center column
is staggered. The ends of the strips won't be
square with each other; they'll be trimmed
later. **(FIGURE 3)**

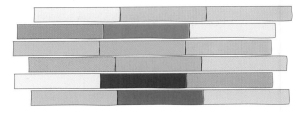

FIGURE 3

4. *join the strips*

Once you are happy with the strip arrangement, pin then sew the strips together as follows: For the wonky look of this quilt, assemble the strips unevenly by arranging the raw edges of each strip so that they are slightly askew, and then sew a straight seam to join the pieces (seam allowances will vary according to your wonkiness). Alternatively, arrange the raw edges evenly but allow your seam allowance to become slightly wider or narrower as you sew across the length of the strip. You may also want to sew with an extra-large allowance on some strips (up to 1" [2.5cm]) so that some strips are narrower than others. **(FIGURE 4)**

Trim the seam allowances to about ¼" (6mm). Press all seam allowances in the same direction, toward one end of the quilt.

5. *trim the edges of the top*

When all the strips are joined together, the edges of the quilt top will be uneven and will need to be made square. Use a quilter's ruler or yardstick and a rotary cutter or scissors to even all the edges and create right angles on all 4 corners.

Measure the finished size of the trimmed quilt top.

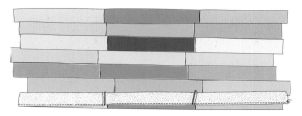

FIGURE 4

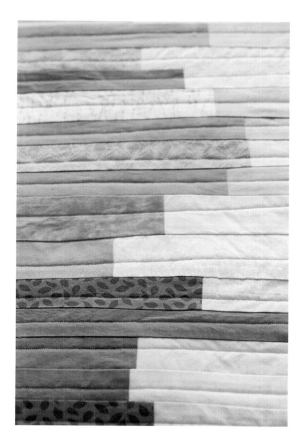

6. layer batting and back

Cut the batting and quilt back fabric 6" (15cm) longer and wider than the quilt top. Lay the quilt back on your work surface right side down, smoothing it to ensure there are no bumps or wrinkles. Lay the batting on top of this, aligning all edges and corners. Center the quilt top, right side up, on top of the batting, sandwiching the batting between the quilt front and quilt back. **(FIGURE 5)**

7. baste

Using a hand-sewing needle and thread, baste all 3 layers of the quilt together (page 21) using long running stitches (approximately 3" [7.5cm] long) placed approximately 6" (15cm) apart. Alternatively, you can pin the layers together with safety pins.

8. quilt

You can now quilt the 3 layers together by hand or machine (page 21).

Using all-purpose thread in a neutral color, quilt all the layers together, making one line of horizontal quilting stitches across each horizontal strip. In keeping with the wonky look of this design, don't worry about making the quilting lines perfectly even—it's fine if they slant or go a bit crooked. **(FIGURE 5)**

9. bind + finish

Remove the basting stitches. Trim the batting and quilt back so that they are even with the raw edges of the quilt top.

Finish the quilt's raw edges with quilt binding (page 22).

FIGURE 5

PERSONALIZE IT!

It's really easy to change up this design with different colors or a different layout. I think it would look great if the center column were shades of all one color, like blues or browns. It would also be fun to stagger the color sections in a different configuration, such as in a diagonal column instead of vertical.

60-second *hello*

Got a minute? Stitch up these cute greeting cards with your fabric scraps.

supplies

* Basic sewing supplies (page 11)
* Medium-weight fabric scraps
* Blank greeting cards
* Adhesive such as double-sided tape, glue, or double-sided fusible webbing

1. Randomly stitch together strips of scrap fabric to create a patchwork piece that is slightly larger than the front of your card, and press all seams to one side. Or, simply select a solid piece of fabric that is at least the size of your card.

2. Trim the fabric to just slightly smaller than the front of your card.

3. To prevent shifting while sewing, attach the fabric to the card with an adhesive of your choice. (If you are using glue, allow it to dry before proceeding.)

4. Topstitch (page 17) all 4 sides of the fabric, making sure the card is open flat so you don't sew it closed.

quick, cute gifts

9-to-5 *folder*

Tuck business cards, a pen, notes, and more into the pockets of this **handy portfolio**. I used suiting fabric for the exterior to give it an office-y touch, but this piece would look *fantastic* in a colorful print, too.

finished dimensions
WIDTH: 6" (15cm) closed,
16½" (42cm) open
LENGTH: 9" (23cm)

supplies
* Basic sewing supplies (page 11)
* ⅓ yard (30cm) medium-weight fabric for exterior
* ¼ yard (23cm) contrasting medium-weight fabric for pockets
* ⅓ yard (30cm) heavyweight fusible interfacing
* Two 1" (2.5cm) buttons
* 7" (18cm) length ⅛"- (3mm-) thick elastic cord
* Plastic folder from office supply store (see Note)

note
To stiffen this piece, flexible plastic inserts are placed in between the layers of fabric. I used a plastic office folder for this, which is the perfect weight and easy to cut with scissors.

1. measure + cut

EXTERIOR, INTERIOR, AND INTERFACING: From the exterior fabric, cut 2 rectangles measuring 10" x 17½" (25.5cm x 44.5cm); cut 2 rectangles the same size from the interfacing.

POCKETS: From the pocket fabric, cut one rectangle 13' x 17½" (33cm x 44.5cm) and one rectangle 7" x 17¾" (18cm x 45cm).

PLASTIC INSERTS: From the plastic, cut 2 rectangles 8¼" x 5½" (21cm x 14cm) and one rectangle 8¼" x 2¾" (21cm x 7cm). **(FIGURE 1)**

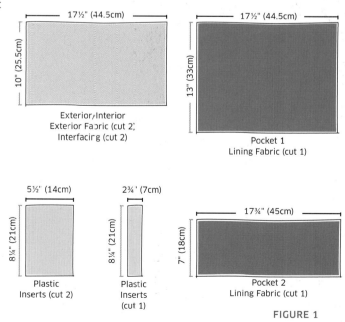

17½" (44.5cm)

10" (25.5cm)

Exterior/Interior
Exterior Fabric (cut 2)
Interfacing (cut 2)

17½" (44.5cm)

13" (33cm)

Pocket 1
Lining Fabric (cut 1)

5½" (14cm)

8¼" (21cm)

Plastic
Inserts (cut 2)

2¾' (7cm)

8¼" (21cm)

Plastic
Inserts
(cut 1)

17¾" (45cm)

7" (18cm)

Pocket 2
Lining Fabric (cut 1)

FIGURE 1

2. attach interfacing

Fuse a piece of interfacing to both 10" x 17½" (25.5cm x 44.5cm) exterior and interior rectangles (page 19).

3. assemble pocket piece

Fold each pocket piece in half lengthwise with wrong sides together and press. Topstitch (page 17) each piece close to the fold.

MAKE THE PENCIL POCKET: Orient the shorter (7" [18cm]) pocket with the folded edge at the top. Mark the bottom raw edge as follows: Measure 3" (7.5cm) in from the left raw edge and mark point **A**. Measure 1" (2.5cm) to the right of **A** and mark point **B**. (FIGURE 2)

Position the shorter pocket on top of the taller (13" [33cm]) pocket, with raw edges aligned, making a small pleat between points **A** and **B** (on the shorter pocket), pleating just enough to align the raw side edges of both pockets. Pin together.

Topstitch the 2 pockets together at point **A**, stitching a vertical line from the bottom raw edge up to the folded top edge of the shorter pocket. Repeat at point **B**. (FIGURE 2)

ATTACH THE POCKETS TO THE INTERIOR OF THE FOLDER: Layer the joined pockets right side up on the right side of one of the 10" x 17½" (25.5cm x 44.5cm) rectangles, aligning the bottom and side edges; pin. Sew together along the sides and bottom, using a ¼" (6mm) seam allowance, leaving the top edge open. This is the interior.

4. attach the elastic cord and buttons

ELASTIC CORD AND RIGHT-HAND BUTTON: On the remaining 10" x 17½" (25.5cm x 44.5cm) rectangle (exterior), mark a spot on the right side of the fabric 2" (5cm) from the right-hand (shorter) side edge, centered between the top and bottom (longer) edges. Fold the elastic cord in half with raw ends aligned. Position the raw ends at the mark, and sew back and forth over them several times. Sew a button on at the same mark, directly over the raw ends of the elastic. (FIGURE 3)

LEFT-HAND BUTTON: Mark another point 5" (12.5cm) from the left edge and centered between the top and bottom edges.

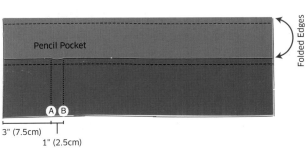

3" (7.5cm)

1" (2.5cm)

Pencil Pocket

Folded Edges

FIGURE 2

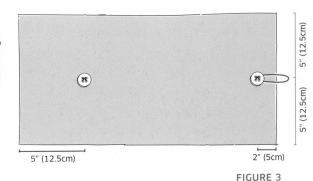

5" (12.5cm)

5" (12.5cm)

5" (12.5cm)

2" (5cm)

FIGURE 3

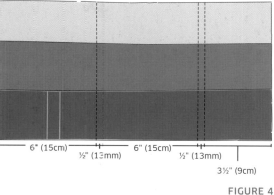

6" (15cm)   ½" (13mm)   6" (15cm)   ½" (13mm)

3½" (9cm)

FIGURE 4

Sew a button at this mark with a thread shank: Place a wooded matchstick (or other object of the same diameter as the elastic) under the button as you sew. Remove the matchstick, pull the button away from the fabric, and wrap the sewing thread around the stitches attaching the button to the fabric 3 times, then bring the thread through the fabric to secure it on the wrong side. **(FIGURE 3)**

5. *assemble the interior and exterior*

Fold under the top edge of the exterior and interior (the edge opposite the pockets) ½" (13mm) and press. Unfold; the fold lines will be used later as a guide.

JOIN THE INTERIOR TO THE EXTERIOR: With right sides together, pin the exterior piece and interior/pocket piece together with all raw edges aligned. Using a heavy-duty needle (since you will be sewing through many layers of fabric), sew the sides and bottom together with a ½" (13mm) seam allowance, leaving the top edge open. Be careful not to catch the elastic loop in the stitching.

Trim the corners (page 19), turn the piece right side out, and use a pointy object to gently poke out the corners; press. Turn the top edges under at the fold lines created earlier, and press.

TOPSTITCH TO MAKE POCKETS: With the interior facing up, measure and mark a point 6" (15cm) from the left-hand side edge, and mark another point ½" (13mm) to the right of this. Measure 6" (15cm) to the right and mark another point, then measure ½" (13mm) to the right of this and mark another point. Topstitch through all layers at each of these 4 points, making a vertical line of stitching from the top edge to the bottom edge. **(FIGURE 4)**.

FINISH: Insert the two 5½"- (14cm-) wide plastic pieces in the 6' (15cm) sections (between the topstitching), and insert the 2¾"- (7cm-) wide plastic piece in the remaining narrow section.

Topstitch around the perimeter of the entire piece, stitching close to the fold, closing the open top edge.

Insert a small notebook into the top pocket on the center panel, if desired. Fold the folder closed and loop the elastic over the other button to secure.

the magic *sewing kit*

Remove the lid from this seemingly simple *little box*, and a hidden sewing kit springs to life! The sides of the box open outward to *reveal* spots for spools of thread or other *notions*, while the center container is perfect for scissors and more. Sewing on a missing button was never so much fun!

finished dimensions

WIDTH: 4½" (11.4cm) closed,
12" (30.5cm) open
LENGTH: 4½" (11.4cm) closed,
12" (30.5cm) open
HEIGHT: 4¼" (11.4cm)

supplies

* Basic sewing supplies (page 11)
* ½ yard (46cm) medium-weight cotton for exterior
* ½ yard (46cm) medium-weight cotton for interior
* ½ yard (46cm) heavyweight fusible interfacing
* Scraps of craft felt
* 1½ yards (1.4m) ¼"- (6mm-) wide elastic
* 1 large sheet of very heavy card stock or book board, at least 12"(30.5cm) x 15"(38cm)
* Hot glue gun

1. *measure + cut*

BASE: Cut one 13" x 13" (33cm x 33cm) square each from the interior and exterior fabrics. Cut 2 squares the same size from the interfacing.

LID: Cut one 7½" x 7½" (19cm x 19cm) square each from the interior and exterior fabrics. Cut 2 squares the same size from the interfacing.

CENTER CONTAINER: Cut two 3½" x 9" (9cm x 23cm) rectangles from the exterior fabric. Cut 2 rectangles the same size from the interfacing.

FELT PIN PADS: Cut eight 1½" x 2" (3.8cm x 5cm) rectangles from the felt.

CARD STOCK: Using a craft knife, straightedge, and cutting mat, cut five 3½" x 3½" (9cm x 9cm) squares. Cut one 4" x 4" (10cm x 10cm) square, and four 4" x ¾" (10cm x 2cm) rectangles. (FIGURE 1)

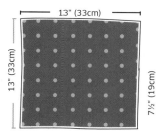

Base
Exterior Fabric (cut 1)
Interior Fabric (cut 1)
Interfacing (cut 2)

Lid
Exterior Fabric (cut 1)
Interior Fabric (cut 1)
Interfacing (cut 2)

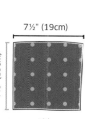

Pin Pads
Felt (cut 8)

Center Container
Exterior Fabric (cut 2)
Interfacing (cut 2)

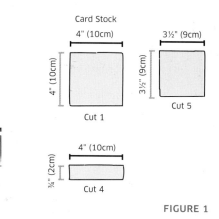

Card Stock

Cut 1

Cut 5

Cut 4

FIGURE 1

2. cut base and lid shapes

BASE: Fuse one piece of corresponding interfacing (page 19) to the wrong side the base exterior and interior pieces. Cut 4" (10cm) square from each corner, creating a plus-sign shape. **(FIGURE 2)**

LID: Fuse one piece of corresponding interfacing to the wrong side of the lid exterior and interior pieces. Cut a 1" (2.5cm) square from each corner, creating a plus-sign shape. **(FIGURE 3)**

the base

3. sew the base

Turn under ½" (13mm) along the outer edge of one "arm" of each base piece (exterior and interior) and press. Open the fold (the folded lines will be used in Step 4).

Pin the 2 base pieces right sides together, aligning all raw edges and the 2 prefolded edges. Leaving the prefolded ends open, sew around all other sides using a ½" (13mm) seam allowance. **(FIGURE 4)**

Clip the seam allowance from all the corners (page 19), taking special care to clip the interior corners as close as possible to the stitch line. Carefully turn the piece right side out and use a pointy tool to gently poke out the corners. Press.

4. add the card stock and elastic to the base

Cut the elastic into eight 5" (12.5cm) lengths. Set aside.

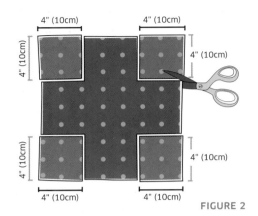

FIGURE 2

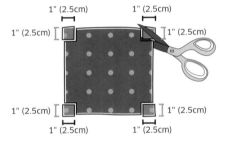

FIGURE 3

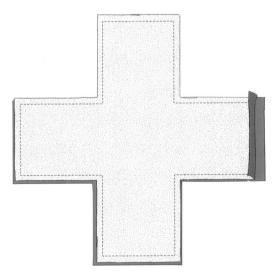

FIGURE 4

Slide one of the 3½" (9cm) squares of card stock through the folded-edge opening, sliding it into one of the other arms. With the lining fabric facing up, place 2 lengths of elastic across the arm, spacing them about 1" (2.5cm) from the outer edge of the arm and about 1" (2.5cm) apart from each other; pin in place. The elastic will overhang ½" (13mm) on each side of the arm. Topstitch (page 17) around all 4 sides of the cardstock, close to the folded edges of the fabric but *outside* the edge of the card stock, stitching across the elastic to anchor it in place. Trim the elastic flush with the edges of the arm after stitching. **(FIGURE 5)**

Repeat for the 2 remaining stitched arms, but not the one with the open edge.

Next, slide a 3½" (9cm) square of card stock into the center area (no stitching is required to hold this piece in place) before sliding the final piece of card stock into the arm with the open edge. Turn under the open edges along the fold lines you made earlier, and press. Add elastic and topstitch around all edges of this arm as you did for the previous arms, closing up the opening.

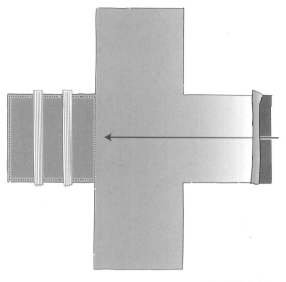

FIGURE 5

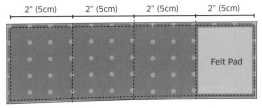

2" (5cm)   2" (5cm)   2" (5cm)   2" (5cm)

Felt Pad

FIGURE 6

Topstitch around the perimeter of the piece. Mark the piece every 2" (5cm) along its length, and sew a vertical line of topstitching at each mark. **(FIGURE 6)**

Fold the piece at the topstitching lines and press. Unfold (the folded lines will be used in Step 6).

the center container

5. sew the center container

Fuse the center container interfacing pieces to the wrong side of the corresponding fabric pieces.

Fold under ½" (13mm) on one short end of each center container piece, and press. Unfold (the folded lines will be used later). With right sides together, pin the 2 pieces together, aligning the prefolded edges and all raw edges. Sew the pieces together around 3 sides with a ½" (13mm) seam allowance, leaving the prefolded edges open.

Clip the seam allowance from the corners and turn the piece right side out. Use a pointy object to gently poke out the corners, and then fold under the prefolded edges. Press.

6. add the felt to the center container

Layer two pieces of felt together and center them on each 2" (5cm) section of the strip made in Step 5. By hand, stitch the felt to the strip with a running stitch (page 15), sewing around all 4 edges of the felt, close to the edge. (Sewing these pieces by machine is not recommended, as the felt tends to shift and distort during machine sewing.)

Fold the strip at each topstitched/folded line from Step 5. By hand, whipstitch (page 15) the 2 open edges together, making a 4-sided column.

Using a hot glue gun, glue one end of the column to the center of the base made in Step 2. (Refer to photo for placement.)

the lid

7. sew the lid

The lid is assembled the using the same basic construction as the base in Step 3 (**FIGURE 4 AND FIGURE 5**).

Turn under ½" (13mm) along the outer edge of one arm of each lid piece and press. Open the fold (this fold line will be used later).

Pin the 2 lid pieces right sides together, aligning the 2 prefolded edges and all raw edges. Leaving the prefolded section open, sew around all other sides using a ½" (13mm) seam allowance.

Clip the seam allowance from all the corners, taking special care to clip the interior corners as close as possible to the stitch line. Turn the piece right side out, using a pointy object to gently poke out the corners, and press.

8. add the card stock to the lid

Slide one of the 4" x ¾" (10cm x 2cm) rectangles of card stock through the open folded edges of the lid, sliding it into one of the other arms. Topstitch around all 4 sides of the card stock, in the space between the edge of the fabric and the card stock. (**FIGURE 7**)

Repeat for 2 more arms, and then slide the 4" (10cm) square of card stock into the center area (no stitching is required to hold this piece in place). Slide the final 4" x ¾" (10cm x 2cm) rectangle of card stock into the arm with the open side. Turn under the open area along the fold lines you made earlier, and press. Topstitch around all edges of this arm as you did for the previous arms.

After assembling, fold up each side of the lid so that the 1" (2.5cm) edges meet at the corners, and whipstitch the sides together at the corners to complete the lid.

9. finish

Fold up all 4 arms of the base and place the lid on top to keep the sewing kit closed. When the lid is off, the sides of the base will fall open and flat. The elastic can be used to hold spools of thread or other notions; fill the center container with small scissors, buttons, or other sewing tools.

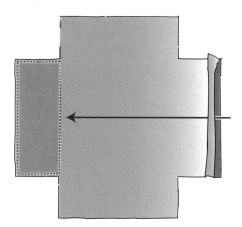

FIGURE 7

quick, cute gifts

on-the-go *jewelry keeper*

Travel in style and stay organized with this handy little case, which allows you **store** all your **accessories** in one place. Snap rings and hoop earrings securely onto the straps, and **stash everything** else in the zipper pockets. Neat!

finished dimensions
WIDTH: 10' (25.5cm)
LENGTH: 4" (10cm) closed,
12" (30.5cm) open

supplies
* Basic sewing supplies (page 11)
* ⅓ yard (30cm) heavyweight fabric such as canvas or cotton twill (for exterior)
* ⅓ yard (30cm) coordinating medium-weight fabric such as quilting cotton (for interior pockets and lining)
* ¼ yard (23cm) coordinating medium-weight fabric such as quilting cotton (for straps)
* Three 8" (20.5cm) zippers
* Five ¼" (6mm) snaps

1. measure + cut
EXTERIOR AND LINING: Cut one 13" x 11" (33cm x 28cm) rectangle from the exterior fabric (for the exterior) and one rectangle of the same size from the lining/pocket fabric.

POCKETS: Cut three 11" x 4" (28cm x 10cm) rectangles and three 11" x 2" (28cm x 5cm) rectangles from the lining/pocket fabric.

STRAPS: Cut three 2" x 8¾" (5cm x 22cm) strips from the strap fabric. **(FIGURE 1)**

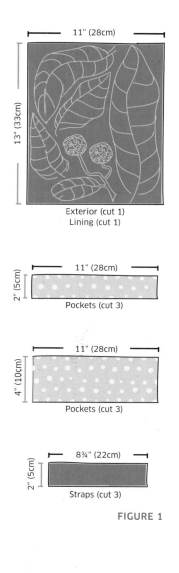

11" (28cm)

13" (33cm)

Exterior (cut 1)
Lining (cut 1)

11" (28cm)

2" (5cm)

Pockets (cut 3)

11" (28cm)

4" (10cm)

Pockets (cut 3)

8¾" (22cm)

2" (5cm)

Straps (cut 3)

FIGURE 1

2. *install the zippers*

With right sides together, align one 11" x 4" (28cm x 10cm) pocket piece with an 11" x 2" (28cm x 5cm) pocket piece, with raw edges aligned along the 11" (28cm) edges. Sew the fabrics together along this edge with a ½" (13mm) seam allowance as follows: Sew with a regular stitch for 1½" (3.8cm), backstitch (page 17) to reinforce, then switch to a basting stitch length and baste for 8" (20.5cm). Switch back to a regular stitch length, backstitch to reinforce, and sew the remaining 1½" (3.8cm). Press the seam allowance open. Repeat for the 2 remaining interior pockets. **(FIGURE 2)**

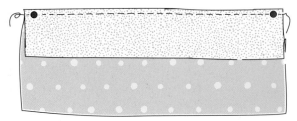

FIGURE 2

Position a zipper right side down on the wrong side of the seam you just sewed, centering the zipper teeth over the basted portion of the seam. Pin it in place. **(FIGURE 3)** Attach the zipper foot to your machine. Topstitch (page 17) along each side of the zipper, about ¼" (6mm) from the teeth, backstitching to reinforce at the beginning and end on each side of the zipper. **(FIGURE 3)** From the right side, carefully remove the basting stitches with a seam ripper.

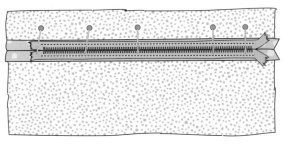

FIGURE 3

Repeat to install the remaining zippers into each of the remaining 2 interior pocket pieces.

3. *join the zipper panels*

Sew the 3 zippered interior-pocket pieces together. With right sides together and the raw edges of the 11" (28cm) sides aligned, pin and sew the pockets together with a ½" (13mm) seam allowance. Press the seam allowances open. **(FIGURE 4)**

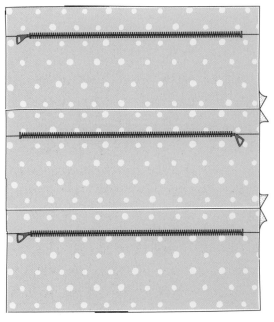

FIGURE 4

4. make and attach the straps

Using the strap pieces cut in Step 1, make 3 straps following the directions on page 20.

Orient the zipper pocket panel, right side up, with the zipper closest to the panel edge at the top. Position one strap 1" (2.5cm) below each zipper, aligning the raw ends of the top and bottom straps with the left-hand raw edge of the pocket panel, and the raw end of the middle strap with the right-hand raw edge of the pocket panel. Sew the straps in place with a ¼" (6mm) seam allowance. Hand-sew a snap to the end of each strap on the underside; sew the corresponding half of the snap to the zipper panel where the strap snap meets it. (**FIGURE 5**)

FIGURE 5

5. sew snaps for the wallet closure

AT THE INSIDE TOP OF THE WALLET: Orient the pocket panel as you did in Step 4. On the top panel, mark placement for the closure snaps 1" (2.5cm) from the top raw edge and 3" (7.5cm) in from each side. Sew a snap at each of these points. **(FIGURE 6)**

AT THE OUTSIDE BOTTOM OF THE WALLET: Mark placement for snaps on the 11" x 13" (28cm x 33cm) exterior panel of the wallet at the opposite end from the snaps you added to the pocket panel above. Mark as follows: Measure 3" (7.5cm) up from the bottom edge of the exterior panel, and 3" (7.5cm) in from each side; mark a point at both locations and sew a snap at each mark. (Be sure to position the snaps at what will be the bottom of the wallet since the corresponding interior snaps were placed at the top of the wallet.) **(FIGURE 7)**

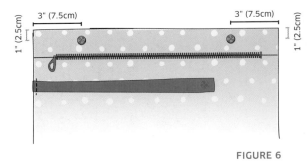

3" (7.5cm)   3" (7.5cm)
1" (2.5cm)   1" (2.5cm)

FIGURE 6

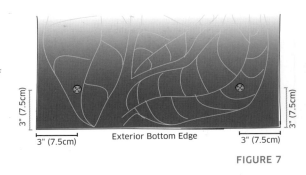

3" (7.5cm)   3" (7.5cm)
Exterior Bottom Edge
3" (7.5cm)   3" (7.5cm)

FIGURE 7

6. join the zipper panel and lining

Place the solid lining panel you cut in Step 1 *right side up* on a flat surface. Layer the pocket panel *right side up* on top of the lining panel matching all raw edges—both pieces will be oriented with the right sides up; pin. Sew together on all 4 sides with a ¼" (6mm) seam allowance. Stitch in the ditch (page 19) in the seams between each pocket panel to create 3 separate compartments. (Layering the fabrics as described here will ensure that you see the right side of the lining fabric when you open the pockets.)

7. join the interior and exterior

Pin the joined pocket/lining panel and exterior panel right sides together, aligning all raw edges. (Be sure to orient them so that the snaps are at the top edge of the lining and the bottom edge of the exterior.). Sew together on all 4 sides with a ½" (13mm) seam allowance, leaving a 5" (12.5cm) opening along the bottom edge for turning the wallet right side out.

Trim the seam allowance at the corners (page 19), and turn the piece right side out. Use a pointy tool to gently poke out corners. Press the seams and whipstitch (page 15) the opening closed by hand.

Fold the wallet in thirds and close with the snaps.

denim *dop bag*

denim *dop bag*

It can be tricky to **sew projects for guys** that they will actually **like**. When it comes to stitching for men, stay away from flashy colors and patterns—basics are the best. This **shave bag** is an essential every man can use, inspired by a classic that never goes out of style: **blue jeans**.

finished dimensions
WIDTH: 4" (10cm)
HEIGHT: 4" (10cm)
LENGTH: 10" (25.5cm)

supplies
* Basic sewing supplies (page 11)
* ¼ yard (23cm) denim
* 9" (23cm) metal zipper
* Heavyweight thread
* Heavy-duty sewing machine needle

tip

Before beginning, load your machine with a heavy-duty needle and heavyweight thread in the bobbin and the needle.

1. *measure + cut*

Cut all pieces from the denim fabric, referring to **FIGURE 1**.

STRAP: Cut one rectangle that is 6" x 4" (15cm x 10cm).

BAG TOP: Cut 2 rectangles that are each 3" x 9" (7.5cm x 23cm) and 2 rectangles that are each 2" x 5" (5cm x 12.5cm).

BAG SIDES AND BOTTOM: Cut 3 rectangles that are each 11" x 5" (28cm x 12.5cm).

BAG ENDS: Cut 2 squares that are each 5" x 5" (12.5cm x 12.5cm).

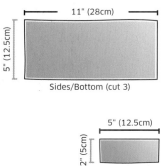

11" (28cm) / 5" (12.5cm)
Sides/Bottom (cut 3)

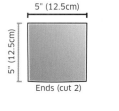

5" (12.5cm) / 5" (12.5cm)
Ends (cut 2)

6" (15cm) / 4" (10cm)
Strap (cut 1)

5" (12.5cm) / 2" (5cm)
Top (cut 2)

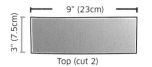

9" (23cm) / 3" (7.5cm)
Top (cut 2)

FIGURE 1

2. *make the strap*

Make the strap following the instructions on page 20. Topstitch (page 17) the strap close to each folded edge. Set the strap aside.

3. *install the zipper on the bag top*

With right sides together, pin the zipper to the long edge on one of the 3" x 9" (7.5cm x 23cm) (top) rectangles. Using a zipper foot, sew the zipper to the fabric close to the teeth. **(FIGURE 2)** Press the seam allowance away from the zipper. Repeat to sew the remaining 3" x 9" (7.5cm x 23cm) rectangle to the other side of the zipper. **(FIGURE 3)** Topstitch on each side of the zipper. **(FIGURE 4)**

The final top piece should be 5" x 9" (12.5cm x 23cm); if necessary, trim your piece to this size before proceeding.

note

When pressing seams near the zipper, be aware that after coming in contact with the iron, the metal zipper will become hot enough to burn you. Be careful!

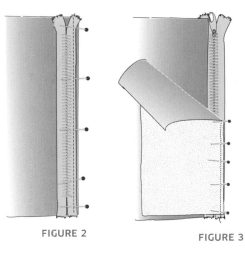

FIGURE 2

FIGURE 3

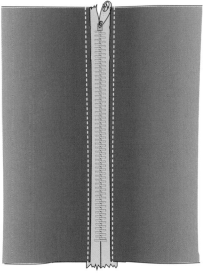

FIGURE 4

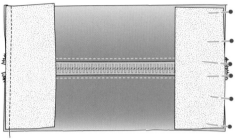

4. finish sewing the bag top

With right sides together, pin a 2" x 5" (5cm x 12.5cm) rectangle to each short end of the zipper top piece. Using a standard presser foot, sew with ½" (13mm) seam allowances. **(FIGURE 5)** Press the seam allowance away from the zipper, and topstitch the seams close to the their edges.

5. add decorative topstitching

Topstitch around all 4 outside edges of the zipper top, sewing ⅝" (16mm) in from the raw edges. **(FIGURE 6)**

On all remaining fabric pieces (sides, bottom, and ends), topstitch around all 4 sides of each piece ⅝" (16mm) in from the raw edges.

6. add the strap to one end

Center and pin the strap on the right side of one end piece, aligning raw edges. Sew the strap to the top with a ¼" (6mm) seam allowance. **(FIGURE 7)**

7. assemble the sides

With right sides together and raw edges aligned, pin the end pieces to the 5" (12.5cm) edges of the side pieces. Sew one edge at a time with a ½" (13mm) seam allowance, *beginning and ending each seam ½" (13mm) from the top and bottom edges.* (This will produce sharp, 3-D corners.) Once all pieces are assembled they will form a rectangle. Press all seams open. **(FIGURE 8)**

FIGURE 5

FIGURE 6

FIGURE 7

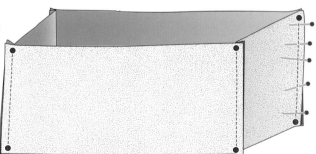

FIGURE 8

8. *attach the bottom*

With right sides together and raw edges aligned, pin and sew the 11" (28cm) edges of the bottom to the 11" (28cm) edges of the sides, leaving ½" (13mm) unsewn at the beginning and end of each seam. Pin and sew the 5" (12.5cm) edges the same way. Press the seam allowances open. **(FIGURE 9)**

Trim the seam allowance at the corners (page 19). Turn the bag right side out and press the seams.

9. *attach the top*

Turn the bag inside out. With the zipper open and right sides together, pin then sew the top to the bag body the same way you did the bottom, leaving ½" (13mm) unsewn at the beginning and end of each seam. Trim the seam allowance at the corners. Turn the bag right side out through the zippered opening and press the seams.

GO HEAVY

Heavyweight thread gives this bag its distinctive 'jeans' look. If you've never used heavy thread before, give it a try—it makes a huge impact in the look of your finished project. Simply load it into your machine as you would all-purpose thread, and stitch away!

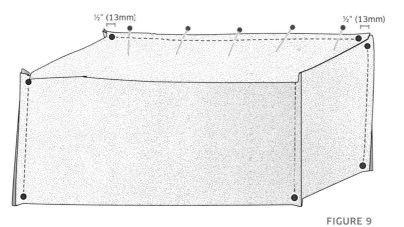

½" (13mm)   ½" (13mm)

FIGURE 9

mister *bunny* & miss *kitty*

This *dapper duo* is all dressed up for a night on the town!
They're stitched in soft wool flannel, making them *irresistibly
cuddly*. You can purchase the flannel by the yard—or even better,
cut up old flannel shirts from the thrift store or your dad's closet.

finished dimensions

BUNNY: Width (across the arms):
14" (35.5cm); height: 20" (51cm)
KITTY: Width (across the arms):
14" (35.5cm); height: 16" (40.5cm)

supplies

* Basic sewing supplies (page 11)
* ⅓ yard (30cm) brown wool flannel (or one large adult flannel shirt)
* ⅛ yard (11cm) plaid wool flannel (or one small flannel shirt)
* ⅓ yard (30cm) gray wool flannel (or one large adult flannel shirt)
* ¼ yard (23cm) white craft felt
* ⅛ yard (11cm) pink craft felt
* ⅛ yard (11cm) black craft felt
* ⅛ yard (11cm) red cotton fabric
* Two 12mm safety eyes
* Two 8mm safety eyes
* Black embroidery floss
* ¼ yard (23cm) fusible web
* One 12-ounce (340g) bag fiberfill
* 7" (18cm) white rickrack
* Three ⅜" (1cm) white buttons

mister bunny

1. measure + cut

Cut the following pieces from the fabrics as indicated. (FIGURE 1)

from brown wool flannel:

Bunny Body (cut 2): 13½" x 10" (34.5cm x 25.5cm). From one of the 10" (25.5cm) edges of these pieces, cut out a centered 6" x 4" (15cm x 10cm) rectangle, as shown (FIGURE 1), to form the ears.
Bunny Feet (cut 2): 5" x 2" (12.5cm x 5cm)
Bunny Arms (cut 2): 5" x 4" (12.5cm x 10cm)

from plaid wool flannel:

Bunny Pants (cut 2): 10" x 4" (25.5cm x 10cm)
Bunny Legs (cut 2): 5" x 4" (12.5cm x 10cm)

from pink craft felt:

Inside Bunny Ears (cut 2): 4" x 1½" (10cm x 3.8cm). Cut each piece into a freehand oblong oval shape with a flat bottom (refer to photo).

from white craft felt:

Bunny Face (cut one): 6" x 5" (15cm x 12.5cm). Cut this piece into a freehand oval shape.

from red cotton:

Bunny Tie (cut one): 2½" x 2½" (6.5cm x 6.5cm)
Bunny Tie Closure (cut one): 1" x 1" (2.5cm x 2.5cm)

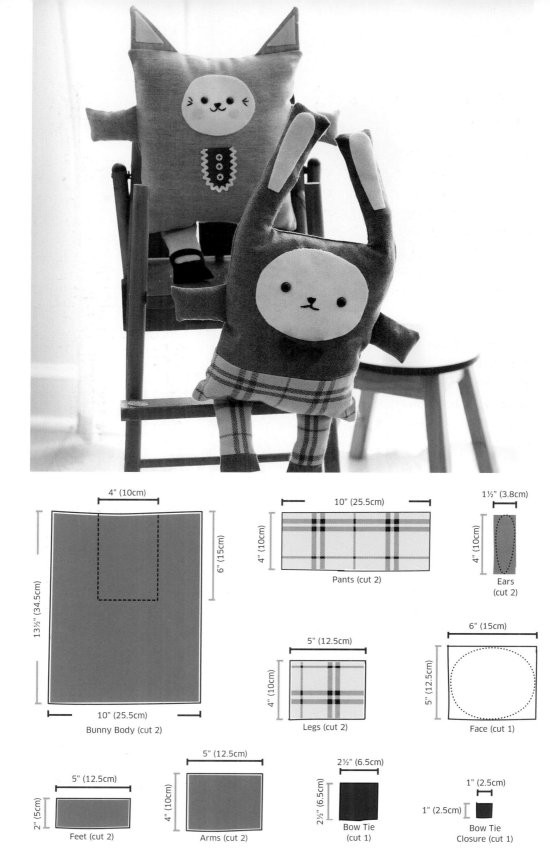

4" (10cm)

6" (15cm)

13½" (34.5cm)

10" (25.5cm)

Bunny Body (cut 2)

10" (25.5cm)

4" (10cm)

Pants (cut 2)

1½" (3.8cm)

4" (10cm)

Ears
(cut 2)

5" (12.5cm)

4" (10cm)

Legs (cut 2)

6" (15cm)

5" (12.5cm)

Face (cut 1)

5" (12.5cm)

2" (5cm)

Feet (cut 2)

5" (12.5cm)

4" (10cm)

Arms (cut 2)

2½" (6.5cm)

2½" (6.5cm)

Bow Tie
(cut 1)

1" (2.5cm)

1" (2.5cm)

Bow Tie
Closure (cut 1)

FIGURE 1 (MISTER BUNNY CUTTING DIAGRAMS)

2. *make the bunny's face and ears*

Refer to **FIGURE 2**.

FACE: On the center of the bunny face oval, sketch a simple nose and mouth, using the photo for guidance. (Don't worry if it's a little crooked or imperfect; that adds to the charm!) Using black embroidery floss, embroider the nose using a satin stitch and the mouth using a split stitch. (See Embroidery Stitches sidebar on page 155 for instructions.)

Cut a piece of fusible web that is slightly smaller than the bunny's face. Sandwich the fusible web between the felt oval and the right side of the body piece, and fuse the face to the body, following the instructions on the fusible web packaging. Refer to the photo for placement.

On the face, mark spots for the eyes on each side of the bunny's nose. With a seam ripper, carefully pierce the fabric at the spots you want to place the eyes.

Following the manufacturer's instructions, install a 12mm eye in each hole, placing the cap on the wrong side of the fabric. (The eyes will be installed through both the face and body layers.)

EARS: Using fusible web, fuse the pink inner ears to the right side of the bunny body front, centering them on the ear portions of the body.

FIGURE 2

FIGURE 3

FIGURE 4

tip

If these toys will be given to a child, I suggest reinforcing the felt ears and face by hand-sewing them to the body. Using a whipstitch (page 15), matching thread, and a hand-sewing needle, simply stitch around the perimeter of the felt.

quick, cute gifts

3. make the bow tie

Fold the 2½" x 2½" (6.5cm x 6.5cm) piece of red cotton in half with right sides together and stitch around 2 sides using a ¼" (6mm) seam allowance, pinning if necesssary. **(FIGURE 3)** Trim corners (page 19), turn right side out, and use a pointy object to gently poke out the corners. Turn under the remaining raw edge ¼" (6mm) and press. Topstitch around all 4 sides. Gather into a bowtie shape by pleating at the center (refer to photo).

Fold the 1" (2.5cm) square of red cotton into thirds and wrap it around the gathered center. Using matching thread and a hand-sewing needle, secure the band at the back of the bowtie, and stitch the bowtie to the bunny's body below his face. **(FIGURE 4)**

4. assemble the bunny

Refer to **FIGURE 2**.

PANTS: With right sides together, pin then sew a pants piece to the bottom of each body piece (front and back) with ½" (13mm) seam allowances. Press the seam allowances to one side.

ARMS: With right sides together, fold each arm piece in half so that the 5" (12.5cm) sides are aligned; pin. With a ½" (13mm) seam

allowance, sew each arm together along the raw 5" (12.5cm) side and one short end, leaving the remaining short end open. Trim the seam allowance at the corners and turn right side out. Use a pointy tool to gently poke out the corners. Press the seams, and stuff the arms lightly with fiberfill.

LEGS AND FEET: With right sides together, align the 5" (12.5cm) edges of each leg and foot piece; pin. Sew together with a ½" (13mm) seam allowance. Press the seam allowances to one side.

Fold the legs in half lengthwise with right sides together; pin then sew with a ½" (13mm) seam allowance along the feet end and up the raw side of the legs. Trim the seam allowance at the corners and turn right side out. Press the seams, and stuff the legs lightly with fiberfill.

ATTACH THE ARMS AND LEGS: Pin the arms to the right side of the front of the body, aligning the raw ends of the arms with the raw edges of the sides of the body, and centering the arms near the bottom of the bunny's face. Pin the legs to the bottom edge of the bunny's body, aligning raw ends and positioning the legs 1½" (3.8cm) in from the corners. Sew the arms and legs in place using a ¼" (6mm) seam allowance.

JOIN THE FRONT AND BACK: Position the front and back together with right sides together and all raw edges aligned (the arms and legs should be facing inward, sandwiched between the body pieces). Pin well to avoid shifting, and sew the 2 pieces together on all sides using a ½" (13mm) seam allowance, and leaving an opening on the bottom edge between the legs. (Be sure to backstitch [page 17] at the beginning and end of the opening to reinforce so the seam doesn't unravel during stuffing.)

STUFF AND FINISH: Trim the seam allowance at the corners, including the interior corners at the base of the ears. Carefully turn the bunny right side out, using a pointy tool to gently poke out the corners, and stuff him with fiberfll. Whipstitch the opening closed.

EMBROIDERY STITCHES

Thread an embroidery needle with 3 strands of embroidery floss for each of these stitches.

* The split stitch creates a continual line of connected stitches that is easy to manipulate around curves, such as for the mouths of the kitty and bunny. Bring the needle up through the threads of the preceding stitch, then insert back into the fabric to complete the next stitch.

* The satin stitch is great for filling in solid areas, such as the kitty and bunny noses. Bring the needle up on one edge of the area you want to fill, and bring it down on the opposite edge. Repeat, making each stitch parallel to the previous, working the stitches very close together, until the entire area is filled in.

miss kitty

1. measure + cut

Cut the following pieces from the fabrics as indicated. (FIGURE 5)

from gray wool flannel:

Kitty Body (cut 2): 11" x 10" (28cm x 25.5cm)
Kitty Arms (cut 2): 4" x 5" (10cm x 12.5cm)
Kitty Legs (cut 2): 5" x 5½" (12.5cm x 14cm)
Kitty Ears (cut 2): 3½" x 3½" (9cm x 9cm)

from pink craft felt:

Kitty Cheeks (cut 2): ¾" x ¾" (2cm x 2cm). Cut each piece into a freehand circle.
Inside Kitty Ears (cut one): 1½" x 1½" (3.8cm x 3.8cm)

from white craft felt:

Kitty Face (cut one): 4" x 3½" (10cm x 9cm). Cut this piece into a freehand oval shape.

from black craft felt:

Kitty Shoes (cut 2): 4½" x 2" (11.5cm x 5cm)

from red cotton:

Kitty Bib (cut one): 1½" x 2½" (3.8cm x 6.5cm). Trim one end of this piece into a curve, as shown.

2. make the kitty's face and bib

FACE: In the center of the kitty's face, sketch a nose and mouth. (Don't worry if it's a little crooked or imperfect, that adds to the charm!) Using black embroidery floss, embroider the nose using a satin stitch and the mouth using a split stitch (see sidebar, page 155).

EYES: Position the eyes on the face and mark their placement with a pen. Don't attach the eyes yet; just mark their position so that you can plan the other facial features. (FIGURE 6)

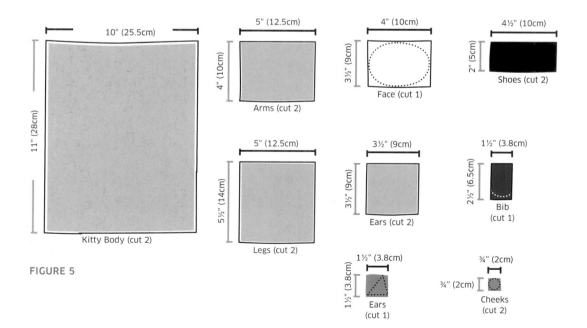

FIGURE 5

Using fusible web, fuse the cheeks to the face below the eyes.

To the sides of the eyes, sketch lines for the whiskers. Embroider the whiskers using a split stitch (page 155).

FUSE THE FACE TO THE BODY: Using fusible web, fuse the face to the kitty's body. Install the eyes at the marked points, carefully piercing through both the felt face and the fabric of the body, and placing the caps of the safety eyes on the wrong side.

Turn under the straight short edge of the bib piece ¼" (6mm). Press and topstitch (page 17) the turned edge. Using fusible web, fuse the bib to the body below the face. With black embroidery floss, sew the 3 buttons onto the bib.

3. *make the kitty's ears, arms, and legs*

Refer to **FIGURE 6**.

EARS: With right sides together, fold each ear piece in half diagonally, and sew along one raw edge with a ½" (13mm) seam allowance. Clip the seam allowance at the corner (page 19). Turn the ears right side out and use a pointy tool to gently poke out the corners; press.

PINK OF EARS: Cut the 1½" (3.8cm) square of pink felt in half diagonally to form the 2 triangles for the pink of the ears. Using fusible web, fuse one triangle to the front of each ear. Be sure to flip the ears before fusing so that the slanted side will face to the interior for each ear, as shown.

ARMS: With right sides together, fold each arm piece in half so that the 5" (12.5cm) sides are aligned; pin. With a ½" (13mm) seam allowance, sew each arm together along the raw 5" (12.5cm) side and one short end, leaving the remaining short end open. Trim the seam allowance at the corners, turn right side out, and use a pointy tool to gently poke out the corners. Press the seams, and stuff the arms lightly with fiberfill.

LEGS: With right sides together, fold each leg in half lengthwise with raw edges aligned; pin. With a ½" (13mm) seam allowance, sew the legs together along the 5½" (14cm) side and one short end, leaving the remaining short end open. Trim the seam allowance at the corners and turn right side out and poke out the corners. Press the seams, and stuff the legs lightly with fiberfill.

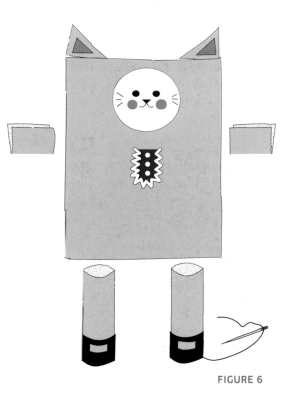

FIGURE 6

4. *make the kitty's shoes*

To make the opening in the shoes, fold each shoe piece in half with the 2" (5cm) ends aligned. On the fold, about ½" (13mm) in from one edge, make a half-oval cut about ½" (13mm) long and ½" (13mm) deep. Unfold the piece; you'll have an oval opening about 1" (2.5cm) long and ½" (13mm) deep. **(FIGURE 7)**

For each shoe piece, bring the 2" (5cm) ends together to form a loop. Whipstitch (page 15) the 2" (5cm) ends together. Slip the shoes onto the legs and whipstitch the bottom closed, catching the fabric of the legs in some of the stitches to anchor the shoes in place.

5. *assemble miss kitty*

Refer to **FIGURE 6**.

ATTACH THE ARMS, LEGS, AND EARS: With right sides together, pin the arms to the body front, aligning the raw ends of the arms with the raw ends of the sides of the body, and centering the arms between the kitty's face and bib. With right sides together, pin the legs to the bottom edge of the kitty's body, aligning the raw ends and positioning the legs 1½" (3.8cm) in from the corners. Pin the ears to the top of the body, ½" (13mm) in from the corners, with the points of the ears on the outside.

Sew the arms, legs, and ears in place using a ¼" (6mm) seam allowance.

JOIN THE FRONT AND BACK: Position the front and back together with right sides together and all raw edges aligned (the arms, legs, and ears should be facing inward, sandwiched between the body pieces). Pin well to avoid shifting, and sew the front and back pieces

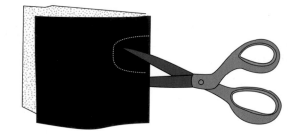

FIGURE 7

together on all sides using a ½" (13mm) seam allowance, leaving an opening on the bottom edge between the legs for stuffing. Be sure to backstitch at the beginning and end of this seam to reinforce so the stitching doesn't unravel during stuffing.

STUFF AND FINISH: Trim the seam allowance at the corners. Carefully turn the kitty right side out, use a pointy tool to gently poke out the corners, and stuff her with fiberfill. Whipstitch the opening closed.

Using fabric glue, glue the rickrack around the sides and curved edge of the bib.

 *GO GREEN!*

Old clothing is a fantastic source of fabric for new sewing projects. Scour the thrift store or your own closets for pieces to harvest. (The men's section in thrift stores is a great place to start, as the garments are usually larger and sometimes the dressier pieces are barely worn.)

To get the most from your garments, wash and dry them after you bring them home. Cut apart the garment at the seams, being careful to preserve as much surface area as possible. Cut off all the buttons and add them to your button stash. Finally, sort your fabric pieces by color and fiber, and your collection of upcycled fabrics will be ready and waiting for the sewing machine!

fabric resources

Choice of fabric is key when it comes to sewing success.
Here are my favorite sources, in New York City and online,
for finding killer materials. (You can shop all the New York City
stores on the web, too.)

where I shop for fabric in new york city

MOOD FABRICS
225 West 37th Street
New York, NY 10018-5703
www.moodfabrics.com
It's where the **Project Runway**
cast members shop, and I too
spent many, many days here
while making this book. Their
fabric selection is, quite simply,
a dream.

B&J FABRICS
525 7th Avenue
New York, New York 10018
www.bandjfabrics.com
A must-stop when fabric
shopping in New York City, this
store stocks everything from
quilting fabrics to garment
materials.

M&J TRIMMING
1008 6th Avenue
New York, NY 10018
www.mjtrim.com
This legendary New York shop
has every trim, ribbon, and
button a sewer could ever want.

IKEA
www.ikea.com
I never cease to be amazed at
how cool Ikea's fabrics are; most
are heavy decorator weight in
bold patterns.

PURL SOHO
459 Broome Street
New York, NY 10013
www.purlsoho.com
An amazing online and brick-
and-mortar shop with a
wonderful collection of fabrics.

THE CITY QUILTER
133 West 25th Street
New York, NY 10001
www.thecityquilter.com
This is the only hardcore quilting
shop in New York City, and I stop
here often for everything I need.

great online sources

WWW.SUPERBUZZY.COM
This web site stocks a truly
irresistible selection of Japanese
fabrics, notions, and supplies.

WWW.PHATFABRIC.COM
A great place to browse for cool
fabrics that you might not find in
your local shops.

WWW.ETSY.COM
Check here for lots of unique
fabrics (such as hand-printed
indie options); individual sellers
stock their shop with commercial
fabrics, too.

WWW.REPRODEPOT.COM
This site features vintage fabrics
as well as vintage reproductions.

WWW.SEWZANNESFABRICS.
COM
A good place to look for
charming children's prints.

WWW.FABRICWORM.COM
A fantastic site for modern
fabrics, especially quilting
cottons.

index Note: Page numbers in *italics* indicate projects